Reader's Digest
Super
Salads

Reader's Digest

Super
Salads

Published by The Reader's Digest Association Limited
London • New York • Sydney • Montreal

Super Salads is part of a series of cookery books called
Eat Well Live Well and was created by Amazon Publishing Limited.

Series Editor *Norma MacMillan*
Volume Editor *Felicity Jackson*
Art Director *Ruth Prentice*
Photographic Direction *Ruth Prentice, Alison Shackleton*
DTP *Peter Howard*
Editorial Assistant *Jasmine Brown*
Nutritionists *Moya de Wet, BSc Hons (Nutri.), A. Dip. Dietetics,
Fiona Hunter, BSc Hons (Nutri.), Dip. Dietetics*

Contributors
Writers *Catherine Atkinson, Sara Buenfeld, Carole Clements,
Linda Collister, Beverly LeBlanc, Sara Lewis, Marlena Spieler, Judith Wills*
Recipe Testers *Catherine Atkinson, Maggie Pannell, Anne Sheasby, Gina Steer*
Photographers *Martin Brigdale, Gus Filgate, William Lingwood*
Stylist *Helen Trent*
Home Economists *Julie Beresford, Joanna Farrow, Annabel Ford,
Bridget Sargeson, Linda Tubby, Sunil Vijayakar, Berit Vinegrad*

For Reader's Digest
Project Editor *Rachel Warren Chadd*
Project Art Editor *Louise Turpin*
Reader's Digest General Books
Editorial Director *Cortina Butler*
Art Director *Nick Clark*
Series Editor Christine Noble

Paperback edition 2004
Paperback Art Editor *Jane McKenna*

ISBN 0 276 42801 3

First Edition Copyright © 2001
The Reader's Digest Association Limited
11 Westferry Circus, Canary Wharf, London E14 4HE
www.readersdigest.co.uk

Copyright © 2001 Reader's Digest Association Far East Limited
Philippines copyright © 2001 Reader's Digest Association Far East Limited

We are committed to both the quality of our products and the service we
provide to our customers. We value your comments, so please feel free to
contact us on 08705 113366, or by email at cust_service@readersdigest.co.uk
If you have any comments about the content of our books, you can contact us
at: gbeditorial@readersdigest.co.uk

Notes for the reader
• Use all metric or all imperial measures when preparing a recipe,
as the two sets of measurements are not exact equivalents.
• Recipes were tested using metric measures and conventional (not
fan-assisted) ovens. Medium eggs were used, unless otherwise
specified.
• Can sizes are approximate, as weights can vary slightly according
to the manufacturer.
• Preparation and cooking times are only intended as a guide.

The nutritional information in this book is for reference only.
The editors urge anyone with continuing medical problems or
symptoms to consult a doctor.

Contents

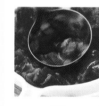

50
Warm Salads

82
Substantial Salads

104
Special Salads

132
Salads on the Side

Eating well to live well

Eating a healthy diet can help you look good, feel great and have lots of energy. Nutrition fads come and go, but the simple keys to eating well remain the same: enjoy a variety of food – no single food contains all the vitamins, minerals, fibre and other essential components you need for health and vitality – and get the balance right by looking at the proportions of the different foods you eat. Add some regular exercise too – at least 30 minutes a day, 3 times a week – and you'll be helping yourself to live well and make the most of your true potential.

Getting it into proportion

Current guidelines are that most people in the UK should eat more starchy foods, more fruit and vegetables, and less fat, meat products and sugary foods. It is almost impossible to give exact amounts that you should eat, as every single person's requirements vary, depending on size, age and the amount of energy expended during the day. However, nutrition experts have suggested an ideal balance of the different foods that provide us with energy (calories) and the nutrients needed for health. The number of daily portions of each of the food groups will vary from person to person – for example, an active teenager might need to eat up to 14 portions of starchy carbohydrates every day, whereas a sedentary adult would only require 6 or 7 portions – but the proportions of the food groups in relation to each other should ideally stay the same.

More detailed explanations of food groups and nutritional terms can be found on pages 156–158, together with brief guidelines on amounts which can be used in conjunction with the nutritional analyses of the recipes. A simple way to get the balance right, however, is to imagine a daily 'plate' divided into the different food groups. On the imaginary 'plate', starchy carbohydrates fill at least one-third of the space, thus constituting the main part of your meals. Fruit and vegetables fill the same amount of space. The remaining third of the 'plate' is divided mainly between protein foods and dairy foods, with just a little space allowed for foods containing fat and sugar. These are the proportions to aim for.

It isn't essential to eat the ideal proportions on the 'plate' at every meal, or even every day – balancing them over a week or two is just as good. The healthiest diet for you and your family is one that is generally balanced and sustainable in the long term.

Our daily plate

Starchy carbohydrate foods: eat 6–14 portions a day
At least 50% of the calories in a healthy diet should come from carbohydrates, and most of that from starchy foods – bread, potatoes and other starchy vegetables, pasta, rice and cereals. For most people in the UK this means doubling current intake. Starchy carbohydrates are the best foods for energy. They also provide protein and essential vitamins and minerals, particularly those from the B group. Eat a variety of starchy foods, choosing wholemeal or wholegrain types whenever possible, because the fibre they contain helps to prevent constipation, bowel disease, heart disease and other health problems.
What is a portion of starchy foods?
Some examples are: 3 tbsp breakfast cereal • 2 tbsp muesli • 1 slice of bread or toast • 1 bread roll, bap or bun • 1 small pitta bread, naan bread or chapatti • 3 crackers or crispbreads • 1 medium-sized potato • 1 medium-sized plantain or small sweet potato • 2 heaped tbsp boiled rice • 2 heaped tbsp boiled pasta.

Fruit and vegetables: eat at least 5 portions a day
Nutrition experts are unanimous that we would all benefit from eating more fruit and vegetables each day – a total of at least 400 g (14 oz) of fruit and vegetables (edible part) is the target. Fruit and vegetables provide vitamin C for immunity and healing, and other 'antioxidant' vitamins and minerals for protection against cardiovascular disease and cancer. They also offer several 'phytochemicals' that help protect against cancer, and B vitamins, especially folate, which is important for women planning a pregnancy, to prevent birth defects. All of these, plus other nutrients, work together to boost well-being.

Antioxidant nutrients (e.g. vitamins C and beta-carotene, which are mainly derived from fruit and vegetables) and vitamin E help to prevent harmful free radicals in the body initiating or accelerating cancer, heart disease, cataracts, arthritis, general ageing, sun damage to skin, and damage to sperm. Free radicals occur naturally as a by-product of normal cell function, but are also caused by pollutants such as tobacco smoke and over-exposure to sunlight.
What is a portion of fruit or vegetables?
Some examples are: 1 medium-sized portion of vegetables or salad • 1 medium-sized piece of fresh fruit • 6 tbsp (about 140 g/5 oz) stewed or canned fruit • 1 small glass (100 ml/3½ fl oz) fruit juice.

Dairy foods: eat 2–3 portions a day
Dairy foods, such as milk, cheese, yogurt and fromage frais, are the best source of calcium for strong bones and teeth, and important for the nervous system. They also provide some protein for growth and repair, vitamin B_{12}, and vitamin A for healthy eyes. They are particularly valuable foods for young children, who need full-fat versions at least up to age 2. Dairy foods are also especially important for adolescent girls to prevent the development of osteoporosis later in life, and for women throughout life generally.

To limit fat intake, wherever possible adults should choose lower-fat dairy foods, such as semi-skimmed milk and low-fat yogurt.
What is a portion of dairy foods?
Some examples are: 1 medium-sized glass (200 ml/7 fl oz) milk • 1 matchbox-sized piece (40 g/1½ oz) Cheddar cheese • 1 small pot of yogurt • 125 g (4½ oz) cottage cheese or fromage frais.

Protein foods: eat 2–4 portions a day

Lean meat, fish, eggs and vegetarian alternatives provide protein for growth and cell repair, as well as iron to prevent anaemia. Meat also provides B vitamins for healthy nerves and digestion, especially vitamin B_{12}, and zinc for growth and healthy bones and skin. Only moderate amounts of these protein-rich foods are required. An adult woman needs about 45 g of protein a day and an adult man 55 g, which constitutes about 11% of a day's calories. This is less than the current average intake. For optimum health, we need to eat some protein every day.

What is a portion of protein-rich food?

Some examples are: 3 slices (85–100 g/3–3½ oz) of roast beef, pork, ham, lamb or chicken • about 100 g (3½ oz) grilled offal • 115–140 g (4–5 oz) cooked fillet of white or oily fish (not fried in batter) • 3 fish fingers • 2 eggs (up to 7 a week) • about 140 g/5 oz baked beans • 60 g (2¼ oz) nuts, peanut butter or other nut products.

Foods containing fat: 1–5 portions a day

Unlike fruit, vegetables and starchy carbohydrates, which can be eaten in abundance, fatty foods should not exceed 33% of the day's calories in a balanced diet, and only 10% of this should be from saturated fat. This quantity of fat may seem a lot, but it isn't – fat contains more than twice as many calories per gram as either carbohydrate or protein.

Overconsumption of fat is a major cause of weight and health problems. A healthy diet must contain a certain amount of fat to provide fat-soluble vitamins and essential fatty acids, needed for the development and function of the brain, eyes and nervous system, but we only need a small amount each day – just 25 g is required, which is much less than we consume in our Western diet. The current recommendations from the Department of Health are a maximum of 71 g fat (of this, 21.5 g saturated) for women each day and 93.5 g fat (28.5 g saturated) for men. The best sources of the essential fatty acids are natural fish oils and pure vegetable oils.

What is a portion of fatty foods?

Some examples are: 1 tsp butter or margarine • 2 tsp low-fat spread • 1 tsp cooking oil • 1 tbsp mayonnaise or vinaigrette (salad dressing) • 1 tbsp cream • 1 individual packet of crisps.

Foods containing sugar: 0–2 portions a day

Although many foods naturally contain sugars (e.g. fruit contains fructose, milk lactose), health experts recommend that we limit 'added' sugars. Added sugars, such as table sugar, provide only calories – they contain no vitamins, minerals or fibre to contribute to health, and it is not necessary to eat them at all. But, as the old adage goes, 'a little of what you fancy does you good' and sugar is no exception. Denial of foods, or using them as rewards or punishment, is not a healthy attitude to eating, and can lead to cravings, binges and yo-yo dieting. Sweet foods are a pleasurable part of a well-balanced diet, but added sugars should account for no more than 11% of the total daily carbohydrate intake.

In assessing how much sugar you consume, don't forget that it is a major ingredient of many processed and ready-prepared foods.

What is a portion of sugary foods?

Some examples are: 3 tsp sugar • 1 heaped tsp jam or honey • 2 biscuits • half a slice of cake • 1 doughnut • 1 Danish pastry • 1 small bar of chocolate • 1 small tube or bag of sweets.

Too salty

Salt (sodium chloride) is essential for a variety of body functions, but we tend to eat too much through consumption of salty processed foods, 'fast' foods and ready-prepared foods, and by adding salt in cooking and at the table. The end result can be rising blood pressure as we get older, which puts us at higher risk of heart disease and stroke. Eating more vegetables and fruit increases potassium intake, which can help to counteract the damaging effects of salt.

Alcohol in a healthy diet

In recent research, moderate drinking of alcohol has been linked with a reduced risk of heart disease and stroke among men and women over 45. However, because of other risks associated with alcohol, particularly in excessive quantities, no doctor would recommend taking up drinking if you are teetotal. The healthiest pattern of drinking is to enjoy small amounts of alcohol with food, to have alcohol-free days and always to avoid getting drunk. A well-balanced diet is vital because nutrients from food (vitamins and minerals) are needed to detoxify the alcohol.

Water – the best choice

Drinking plenty of non-alcoholic liquid each day is an often overlooked part of a well-balanced diet. A minimum of 8 glasses (which is about 2 litres/3½ pints) is the ideal. If possible, these should not all be tea or coffee, as these are stimulants and diuretics, which cause the body to lose liquids, taking with them water-soluble vitamins. Water is the best choice. Other good choices are fruit or herb teas or tisanes, fruit juices – diluted with water, if preferred – or semi-skimmed milk (full-fat milk for very young children). Fizzy sugary or acidic drinks such as cola are more likely to damage tooth enamel than other drinks.

As a guide to the vitamin and mineral content of foods and recipes in the book, we have used the following terms and symbols, based on the percentage of the daily RNI provided by one serving for the average adult man or woman aged 19–49 years (see also pages 156–158):

✓✓✓	or excellent	at least 50% (half)
✓✓	or good	25–50% (one-quarter to one-half)
✓	or useful	10–25% (one-tenth to one-quarter)

Note that recipes contribute other nutrients, but the analyses only include those that provide at least 10% RNI per portion. Vitamins and minerals where deficiencies are rare are not included.

V denotes that a recipe is suitable for vegetarians.

Salad Sensations

An enjoyable way to eat good food

Salads are the ultimate in healthy dishes as they can be prepared from such a wide variety of foods, all of them contributing their own vital nutrients and offering a wonderful range of flavours, colours and textures. Salads can be as light or substantial, as simple or as extravagant as you like, served warm or crisply chilled to suit the occasion and the weather. They make tempting starters, well-balanced main meals and great side dishes. All kinds of everyday ingredients can be transformed into something memorable by mixing them with fresh salad leaves and vegetables, and tossing them with a delicious creamy dressing or a palate-tingling vinaigrette.

Salads in a healthy diet

Not many years ago, a salad was often no more than tomato and cucumber mixed with a few bland lettuce leaves on the side of the plate. Now, with a vast and tempting array of ingredients from all over the world to choose from, a salad can be almost whatever we want it to be – not least, an enjoyable way to stay healthy.

Why salads are so healthy

Nutritionist experts agree that a varied diet is one of the best routes to good health. Salads are a delicious way to enjoy a wide variety of foods, as they can be prepared from all kinds of fruit and vegetables, along with many other ingredients, so they can offer a broad range of nutrients. And because they are so adaptable, suitable for main meals as well as side dishes, perfect for entertaining and great for everyday family meals, salads can be a regular part of everyone's diet.

Current healthy eating guidelines recommend that we should eat at least 5 portions of fruit and vegetables every day. A salad is an easy and tasty way to help you reach this target. Salad is also very nutritious, because the fruit and vegetables are normally used raw, or only lightly cooked, thus retaining maximum vitamins and minerals – for example, the vitamin C content is higher in raw fruit and vegetables than when they are cooked. An added benefit is that raw foods take more chewing and digesting, so they can help to prevent overeating.

Starchy carbohydrates, such as pasta, rice, starchy grains, bread and potatoes, are another important part of a healthy diet, and they are easy to incorporate into a salad. And with the addition of a moderate amount of protein-rich food, such as meat, chicken, fish, cheese, eggs, nuts or pulses, a salad can become a substantial, well-balanced main dish.

What salad nutrients can do

Because salads can contain such a wide range of ingredients, the nutrients on offer will vary from recipe to recipe. All salads, though, supply lots of vitamins, minerals and dietary fibre from their vegetable and fruit content. Among the key nutrients provided are the antioxidants vitamin C and beta-carotene. Antioxidants help to slow down the production of damaging free radicals. Experts believe that a surplus of these free radicals is one of the major causes of coronary heart disease and cancer.

Eating lots of vitamin C-rich fruit and vegetables has other benefits too, such as increasing the absorption of iron from foods eaten at the same time. And beta-carotene is converted by the body into vitamin A, needed for growth. Vitamin E, another antioxidant vitamin found in some vegetables, helps to keep the skin healthy. Most salad leaves are a good source of folate (a B vitamin), which is important in pregnancy to help prevent birth defects.

Fruit and vegetables contain fibre, which is vital for good health. One type, soluble fibre, helps to regulate the levels of cholesterol and sugar in the blood, and has been shown to improve control of late-onset diabetes. Insoluble fibre (plus water) speeds food through the digestive process, helping to prevent constipation and some diseases. Foods containing soluble fibre are also a good source of oligosaccharides, which are substances that stimulate the growth of beneficial bacteria in the gastro-intestinal tract.

Other ingredients in a fresh salad can provide additional important nutrients, such as omega-3 fatty acids (from oily fish and nuts), iron (from red meat), calcium (from cheese and other dairy products) and zinc (from shellfish).

Salads for all seasons

Salads aren't just for summer – they can be warm and hearty, spicy and cheering, just as appetising in January as in July. By using seasonal ingredients, such as asparagus in May and June, or chicory and pumpkin in the autumn, you will ensure maximum taste and nutrients all year round. And you can ring the changes, whatever the season, with the addition of fresh herbs and flavouring ingredients like garlic, chilli and ginger.

◄ Best for B vitamins – meat, poultry, whole grains, cheese, nuts, seeds, eggs and fish; pulses are another good source

▼ Best for beta-carotene – orange-fleshed melons, pumpkin, carrots, dark green leafy vegetables, tomatoes, red peppers, papaya and mango

◄ Best for vitamin C – peppers, green leafy vegetables, citrus fruits, strawberries and kiwi fruit; guava, mango and papaya are other good sources

▼ Best for calcium – dark green leafy vegetables, cheese, yogurt dressings, nuts, seeds, and canned fish with bones

► Best for iron – pulses, liver, lean red meat, wholegrains and dried apricots; other good sources include seeds and dark green, leafy vegetables

► Best for fibre – green leafy vegetables, pears, apples, onions, olives, green beans, dried fruit and fresh berries; other good sources include pulses, whole grains, nuts, asparagus, citrus fruits and mango

A riot of salad leaves

These days a salad can comprise a medley of different leaves, with varying colours, flavours and textures. Greengrocers and supermarkets offer an ever-increasing selection of salad stuffs, ranging from delicate and tender, pale green leaves to vivid red and purplish-brown ones with a robust flavour and crisp texture.

Choosing salad leaves

To be interesting, a leafy salad needs a good mix of colours, flavours and textures. This will also ensure that it is nutritious because, in general, the darker and more bitter leaves tend to have a higher nutrient content than sweet leaves. For example, the darker green (or red) and more strongly flavoured a salad leaf is, the more beta-carotene and other carotenoids it will contain. Also, the dark outer leaves of lettuces may provide up to 50 times more carotenoids than inner, paler leaves. Another way to be sure that leafy salads are nutritious is to make them large. Salad leaves contain such a high proportion of water that you need a lot of them to provide a reasonable amount of nutrients.

Sweet and mild-flavoured leaves

The light, subtle flavour of soft, sweet salad leaves makes them an excellent base for a simple side salad with a tasty vinaigrette, or for salads made with other delicately flavoured ingredients, such as avocado or egg.

Beet greens

Dark green or reddish-green with a red stalk, beet greens taste like a cross between beetroot and spinach – slightly sweet, yet full of flavour. Use young leaves as older ones may be tough. They are rich in carotenoids.

Cos and romaine lettuces

The classic base for a Caesar salad, cos and romaine lettuces have a long, oval head of tightly packed crisp leaves. They are rich in potassium and also contain carotenoids.

Iceberg lettuce

This pale, round, tightly packed lettuce has crisp leaves with a refreshing but bland flavour. It is useful for its texture.

Lamb's lettuce (corn salad, mâche)

These small rosettes of mid-green leaves have a delicious velvety texture and delicate flavour.

Little Gem lettuce

This is a smaller, compact variety of cos lettuce. The rich green outer leaves and delicate yellow inner leaves are crisp, with a sweet flavour. Simply halve or quarter the spear-shaped heads lengthways or separate into individual leaves.

Lollo Rosso lettuce

A non-hearting, loose-leaf lettuce, Lollo Rosso has fringed and crinkled leaves that are tinged deep red at their ends, with a fairly tender yet crisp texture and a bland flavour. It is a useful source of the antioxidant quercetin, which is believed to help to reduce the risk of heart disease.

Oak Leaf lettuce (feuille de chêne)

This loose-leaf lettuce has very attractive serrated, deep bronze leaves and a pleasant mild but distinctive flavour. It is a useful source of the antioxidant quercetin.

Red chard

A member of the beet family, red chard has red stalks and mid to deep-green leaves sometimes tinged with red. It provides fibre, vitamin C, folate and beta-carotene. Use the young leaves in mixed salads to add rich colour.

Round lettuce

With its soft mid-green outer leaves and a slightly crisper, paler heart, this is the traditional 'British lettuce'.

Spinach

Glossy green spinach leaves have a slightly metallic flavour due to their high iron content. The iron is not all absorbed by the body, however, due to the leaf's oxalic acid content. In addition, spinach offers vitamins C and E, folate and a carotenoid called lutein, which aids eye health and may help to protect against lung cancer. Use young leaves raw in salads.

cos, Little Gem and romaine lettuces

round and iceberg lettuces

beet greens

spinach

red chard

lamb's lettuce

Lollo Rosso and Oak Leaf lettuces

chicory

Lollo Biondo and Lollo Verde lettuces

escarole and frisée

mizuna

mustard and cress

Bitter and strongly flavoured leaves

In general, darker salad leaves have a stronger flavour than pale ones, and just a few sprigs of a peppery green such as watercress or rocket will provide delightful contrast in a salad of sweet leaves.

Chicory

Chicory has small, tightly packed, spear-shaped heads of pale – almost white – leaves tinged with yellow or red at the tips. It has a fairly crisp texture and a pleasantly bitter flavour that can be strong. Cut the head into quarters lengthways or separate into individual leaves. Chicory is in season in autumn and winter, so it is an ideal winter salad ingredient. It can be kept in the fridge for up to 5 days.

Escarole

A broad-leaved kind of frisée, this has crunchy, mid-green outer leaves and a pale heart. The flavour is slightly bitter, less bitter than frisée. It is good mixed with milder salad leaves.

Frisée

The large, round, slightly flattened heads of frisée have finely divided, mid-green leaves with a strong bitter flavour. The paler centre leaves are milder.

Lollo Biondo and Lollo Verde lettuces

These loose-leaf lettuces have a fairly mild flavour (but stronger than the closely related Lollo Rosso). If you grow your own loose-leaf lettuces you can pick individual leaves rather than the whole head.

Mizuna

A recent arrival from the Far East, this deeply divided, pretty green leaf has a strong and peppery flavour. It is rich in the B vitamin folate. Mizuna is in season in winter and can add interest to any winter salad. It goes well with sweet flavours such as dried apricots.

Mustard and cress

Sold in small tubs, this mixture of seedlings of garden cress

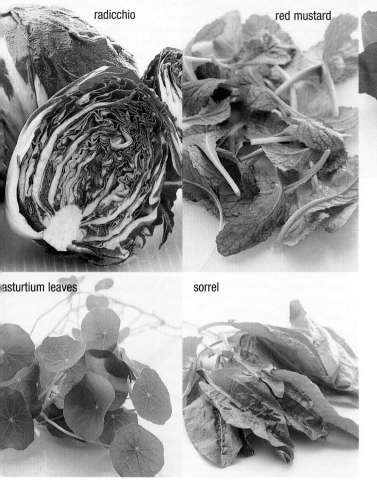

radicchio

red mustard

watercress

rocket

nasturtium leaves

sorrel

Rocket
This popular salad leaf has deep green, elongated frilled leaves with a pungent flavour. It is rich in carotenoids and iron.

Sorrel
Looking something like spinach, sorrel leaves are mid-green and oval or spear shaped. Their flavour is lemony and refreshing, and just a few young leaves will lift a bland salad.

Watercress
The small, glossy, dark green leaves of watercress are rich in vitamin C, folate, iron and other minerals, and carotenoids, and they also offer cancer-fighting glucosinolates. Be sure to use the tender stalks as well as the leaves.

Buying, storing and preparing salad leaves

● Buy the freshest lettuces and salad leaves you can find – the vitamins and minerals are at peak levels when the greens are first harvested. If the leaves have a brown tinge to their edges or are wilted and slimy, don't buy them. Most can be stored in the fridge for up to 4 days, although it is best to use them as soon as possible.

● You may only be able to find some of the less common salad leaves ready-prepared and packed in a cellophane bag, often as part of a mixed salad. Ready-prepared salad leaves should be used within 24 hours, because once cut they begin to lose their vitamin C and B-complex vitamins.

● Give salad leaves a quick wash in cold water, then spin dry in a salad spinner or pat dry in a clean tea-towel. Don't leave them to soak as this will result in the loss of some of the water-soluble vitamins such as C and folate.

● Salad leaves can be trimmed, washed and dried, then kept in the fridge for a few hours before serving, but do not dress them until ready to serve, otherwise the acid in the dressing will make the leaves wilt.

and white mustard (or, sometimes, rape) is mostly used as a garnish or in a sandwich. If eaten in larger quantities, though, it can be a good source of vitamin C and carotenoids.

Nasturtium leaves
With their peppery flavour and nice succulent texture, these make a pretty addition to a mixed leaf salad. They contain phytochemicals, which have antibiotic properties.

Radicchio
A member of the chicory family, radicchio has crisp, deep red and white leaves with a slightly bitter, nutty flavour. It is high in beta-carotene and other cancer-fighting phytochemicals. In season during the autumn, it makes a beautiful addition to a green leaf salad, and is delicious mixed with citrus fruits.

Red mustard
These colourful, mottled red and green leaves have a hot mustardy flavour. If picked as baby leaves, the flavour is milder. Red mustard is a good source of phytochemicals.

salad sensations

15

Salad vegetable variety

When making salads, don't limit yourself to leaves, or to everything raw. Vegetables of all kinds can be used in a salad, and each will contribute its own vitamins, minerals and other beneficial nutrients to the dish.

Making the most of vegetables

Just about any vegetable can be used in a salad, either raw or cooked, to add taste and texture. If lightly boiled or steamed, vegetables retain their colour and crunch; grilling, griddling and roasting bring out a fuller flavour.

Shoots and stalks

Shoots and stalks from the vegetable plant can be anything from baby leeks, asparagus spears and crunchy sticks of celery to fully formed heads of cauliflower and broccoli, and bulbs of fennel. All are delicious in salads.

Artichokes are a delicacy: trimmed, boiled and cooled, they can be served whole dressed with vinaigrette, or the leaves can be discarded and the heart used in a mixed salad. They contain a phytochemical called cynarin, which is said to help control blood cholesterol levels and aid liver function.

Asparagus is best eaten fresh in season (May to June). Whole spears, lightly cooked, can be served cold with vinaigrette and shavings of Parmesan, or used in a salad. To retain maximum nutrients, steam or bake asparagus in foil, and use any juices in the dressing. Asparagus is an excellent source of folate and also provides vitamins A, C and E.

Broccoli florets can be used raw, or cooked until just tender. Purple sprouting broccoli (in season in mid spring), which tastes a little like asparagus, can be cooked in the same way and eaten cold with vinaigrette. Broccoli is an excellent source of folate and vitamin C, and also provides useful amounts of vitamins A (from beta-carotene) and E.

Cabbages, such as red and white cabbage and Chinese leaves, are ideal raw winter salad ingredients. Pak choy and other Chinese cabbages are delicious cooked and used in warm salads. All cabbages are high in vitamin C and B vitamins, in

Shoots and stalks for salads
▶ Cut bulbs of fennel into quarters and trim off the core, then chop or slice. Use the feathery tops as a garnish

◀ Trim the outer leaves from globe artichokes and simmer until tender, then remove the fuzzy choke and chop or slice the heart

▶ Trim and peel kohlrabi, removing all the fibrous underlayer, then grate coarsely. The leaves can be cooked like Swiss chard or spinach

Roots and bulbs for salads

▶ Peel celeriac and cut into chunks, dropping them into water acidulated with lemon juice to prevent them from turning brown. Cut into fine shreds

◀ Simmer or bake sweet potatoes until tender, then slice or chop. Leaving the skin on will boost the fibre content

▶ Trim spring onions, then cut lengthways into thin strips. Chill in iced water to make them curl

particular folate, and in fibre. Red cabbage has lower levels of carotenoids and anti-cancer glucosinolates than white or green cabbages, but it does provide the antioxidant quercetin, which is believed to reduce the risk of heart disease.

Cauliflower can be used in salads in the same way as broccoli. It provides vitamin C and beneficial sulphur compounds.

Celery is a good year-round salad ingredient, normally used raw to contribute crunchy texture. It works well with nuts, citrus fruits, apples, chicken and cheese. It contains potassium and also acts as a diuretic.

Fennel, with its gentle aniseed flavour and crisp texture, is a versatile salad vegetable. Sliced raw it can be used on its own dressed with vinaigrette, or mixed with other ingredients, particularly oranges. Fennel contains phytoestrogens, which are believed to protect against breast and prostate cancers. It is also a good source of potassium.

Kohlrabi, a member of the cabbage family, has purple or green bulbous stems and a delicate turnip-like taste. It can be finely grated and used raw in winter salads, or lightly cooked and added to warm salads. It is a good source of vitamin C.

Leeks can be finely sliced and used raw in salads – they go well with apples, cabbage and nuts – or cooked, cooled and served whole dressed with vinaigrette. Leeks provide vitamin C, folate and carotenoids.

Root and bulb vegetables

Starchy root vegetables such as potatoes and parsnips, bulbs such as beetroot, onions and radishes, and tubers such as carrots and turnips are all excellent salad ingredients, adding their own flavours, textures and valuable nutrients.

Beetroot can be used raw (peeled and grated) or cooked. A valuable source of minerals, including potassium, zinc and iron, it goes well with citrus fruits, peppery leaves such as rocket and watercress, and smoked mackerel.

Carrots add colour as well as sweet flavour to many types of salads – grated, sliced or chopped, or cut into sticks for crudités. The large amount of beta-carotene in carrots make them an excellent source of vitamin A.

Celeriac, with a similar taste to celery, goes well with the same sorts of foods, such as apples, nuts and seeds. It is at its best in winter, when it can be used raw or lightly cooked. It is a source of fibre, vitamin C and potassium.

Onions of all kinds – spring onions, mild Spanish-type onions, red onions, and sweet onions such as Vidalia – can all be used raw in salads. They go well with tomatoes, avocado, peppers and cheese. Onions contain quercetin as well as allicin, which is an antioxidant with anti-fungal and antibiotic properties.

Parsnips, like potatoes, are an excellent source of fibre and starchy carbohydrate, and they can be used like potatoes.

salad sensations

17

Vegetable fruits for salads

◄ Cut butternut squash in half, scoop out the seeds and fibres, and peel thinly. Cut the flesh into chunks and steam until tender

► Shave long strips from courgettes using a swivel vegetable peeler

◄ Wrap wedges of pumpkin in foil and bake until tender, then remove the skin, seeds and fibres, and chop the flesh

► Grill pepper halves, skin side up, until wrinkled and lightly charred. Cool in a polythene bag, then peel

Potatoes, boiled and cooled, can be simply tossed with a herb-flavoured vinaigrette or a creamy dressing or added to mixed salads to provide plenty of good-to-eat, satisfying starch. They are a valuable source of vitamin C and also contribute some iron and B vitamins.

Radishes, both the small, red-skinned ones and the large white radishes called mooli or daikon, can be used raw, sliced or grated, in salads. They provide vitamin C.

Sweet potatoes are a delicious starchy carbohydrate to add to salads. They provide vitamins C and E, potassium and fibre. Orange-fleshed varieties are a good source of beta-carotene.

Turnips can be grated raw and added to salads to give a slightly peppery flavour and crunchy texture, as well as boosting the vitamin C content.

Vegetable fruits

Vegetable fruits add vibrant colour and luscious textures to salads. Some, such as aubergines and sweetcorn, need cooking before using, but many others can be used raw.

Aubergines are best brushed with a little olive oil and baked or grilled, as when fried they soak up large quantities of fat. They can then be dressed with vinaigrette while still warm or left to cool; they work well in salads with tomatoes, onions, peppers and courgettes. Aubergines contain a range of nutrients, though none in large quantities. Their main advantage is that they add bulk while being low in calories.

Avocado is one of the few vegetable fruits with a high fat content; however, most of this is the good monounsaturated type. Avocados are a rich source of vitamin B_6 and also provide vitamins C, E and folate, plus potassium. Use when perfectly ripe for a full flavour and creamy texture. They can be puréed into a dip to serve with crudités, chopped and mixed into a green salad or simply halved and filled with vinaigrette. Avocado flesh will go brown if left in contact with air for long, so prepare just before use.

Broad beans can be cooked and cooled to use in salads. They contain twice as much fibre as green beans and are a good source of the antioxidant quercetin. They also provide vitamins C and E, as well as beta-carotene, which the body can convert to vitamin A.

Courgettes are a versatile salad ingredient as they can be sliced or grated and used raw or cooked. They provide vitamin C, folate and beta-carotene.

Cucumber, being 96% water, makes a refreshing addition to a salad, especially one to accompany a spicy dish such as curry or hot chilli con carne.

Green beans come in many varieties, including fine or French beans, bobby beans and runner beans. Green beans are a significant source of folate and also provide some vitamin C (runner beans offer the most). Lightly cooked, they make a good autumn salad with pulses or with cauliflower and tomatoes. They are a classic addition to salade niçoise.

Mushrooms are delicious marinated in vinaigrette or they can be added raw to mixed salads. They are a good source of B vitamins and they provide copper and potassium. Shiitake mushrooms contain canthaxanthin, a phytochemical that helps to fight cancer.

Peas, when fresh and young, can be added to salads raw, straight from the pod, as can young and tender mange-tout and sugarsnap peas; cooked peas (fresh or frozen) are delicious in rice and pasta salads. Peas are a useful source of vitamin C and fibre, and contribute many B vitamins including folate. Mange-tout and sugarsnap peas are richer sources of vitamin C and fibre because the pods are eaten too.

Peppers can be eaten raw in salads, or stir-fried, grilled or roasted and used warm or cooled – a warm salad of roast Mediterranean vegetables, such as peppers, aubergines, tomatoes and red onions, is always a winner. Peppers are an excellent source of vitamin C (weight for weight, over twice as much as oranges) and contain some vitamin E. Red peppers also offer excellent amounts of beta-carotene.

Pumpkin and other squashes, such as butternut, acorn and patty pan, may seem unusual salad ingredients, but they can make a tasty addition to a rich meat salad, such as duck or beef. Their nutritional benefits vary according to variety, but all squashes provide vitamin A through their beta-carotene content, and some offer vitamin C.

Sweetcorn, in loose kernels and as baby cobs, can be lightly cooked and served in a mixed salad, particularly good in one made with tomatoes and red onion. Sweetcorn contributes dietary fibre, vitamins A, C and folate, and the carotenoid lutein, which is believed to offer smokers some protection against lung cancer. Sweetcorn is also a good source of starchy carbohydrate.

Tomatoes are the world's most popular salad ingredient and rightly so, as they are extremely versatile, delicious in side salads with onions and garlic, watercress, olives, avocado, salad leaves of all kinds and herbs such as basil, and in main course salads with fish such as tuna and sardines, cheeses, chicken and pulses. Used raw, tomatoes are an excellent source of vitamin C and they provide vitamin A from beta-carotene. They also contain a carotenoid compound called lycopene, which acts as an antioxidant, helping to prevent heart disease and some cancers. The lycopene on offer is better absorbed by the body when the tomatoes are cooked, so warm salads that include tomatoes are very nutritious. Another way to enhance lycopene is to add richly flavoured sun-dried tomatoes to salads.

Buying, storing and preparing vegetables

● Buy vegetables as close to preparation and cooking time as you can, otherwise their nutrient content, texture and flavour may suffer.

● Store vegetables in the fridge, except for root vegetables such as potatoes, parsnips and onions, which keep best in a cool, dark and dry place.

● Wash vegetables thoroughly but quickly. Never soak them, because water-soluble vitamins will seep out and then be drained away.

● Prepare vegetables according to the salad you are making. Small chunks are ideal for salsas, larger chunks may be better for main course salads, and slices are good in marinades.

salad sensations

Fruit flavours for salads

Both fresh and dried fruits are a welcome addition to the salad bowl, and not just for dessert. They can be used just as successfully in savoury salads as sweet ones. Most fruits are packed with vitamins, minerals and other nutrients, and are an especially rich source of a variety of disease-fighting phytochemicals.

A refreshing touch

Almost any fruit will make a delicious addition to a salad, contributing flavour, texture, colour and delicate perfume. Oranges, lemons, mangoes and other juicy fruits provide an extra bonus – the juice that escapes from the fruit while it is being prepared can be mixed with oil in place of vinegar, to make a refreshing dressing for the salad.

Favourite fruits

Apples, cherries, grapes and pears are some of the most popular fruits in our diet, and they all make a valuable contribution to good health. Among the many nutrients on offer are flavonoids such as quercetin, which is believed to help to protect against heart disease and stroke.

Apples provide crunch and fresh sweetness to complement strong flavours such as blue cheese. Pears are delicious with bitter leaves like rocket and radicchio, and with pork.

Yellow-orange fruits

Fruits with yellow or orange flesh, such as apricots, mangoes, papaya, canteloupe and Charentais melons, nectarines and peaches, as well as yellow plums, are the best fruit sources of the antioxidant beta-carotene, which can be converted into vitamin A in the body. These fruits also provide many of the B vitamins and vitamin C. Individual fruits within this group have additional nutrients to offer. For example, apricots are a good source of potassium, iron and magnesium, while mangoes provide useful amounts of vitamin E.

Papaya and mango add colour and exotic flavour to rice and pasta salads. Sweet melon is delicious with poultry and salty cheeses such as feta. Apricots and peaches go well in bean salads and those made with bulghur wheat.

Citrus fruits

Grapefruit, kumquats, lemons, limes, oranges, tangerines, pomelos and various other hybrid citrus fruits are some of the richest fruit sources of vitamin C. One medium-to-large orange provides twice the RNI of this vitamin. In addition, pink grapefruit and blood oranges contain good amounts of beta-carotene.

The sweet sharpness of oranges and kumquats goes particularly well in salads with rich game or duck and oily fish. Grapefruit provides a refreshing touch of acidity to balance the sweet taste of lamb. Lemon, lime and other citrus fruit juices make tangy dressings.

Edible flowers in salads

A flower garnish can lift an everyday salad into something unusual and exotic-looking, and many flowers will also add their delicious scent. Edible flowers include nasturtiums, rose petals, borage, pansies, strawberry flowers, and herb flowers such as sage, thyme, rosemary and chives. If you are unsure about whether any other flowers are edible, choose flowers only from the herb garden or check with your local library first. The nutritional value of petals and flower heads is very small as they are used in such tiny quantities, but some flowers, especially herb flowers, offer essential oils and phytochemicals, particularly antioxidants.

salad sensations

20

Berry fruits

Blackberries, red and black currants, blueberries, raspberries, gooseberries, loganberries and strawberries are good sources of many vitamins and fibre. All berries provide vitamin C (blackcurrants are an especially rich source) and vitamin E (blackberries are the richest fruit source of this valuable antioxidant). Strawberries and blackberries also contain the phytochemical ellagic acid, which can help to prevent cancer.

In addition to their use in dessert fruit salads, berry fruits work well in savoury salads. Raspberries are delicious with poultry and rich chicken livers; red and black currants complement seafood and red meat such as beef and duck.

Tropical and exotic fruits

Luscious fruits such as bananas, dates, figs, guavas, kiwi fruit, lychees, passion fruit and granadilla, pomegranate, pineapple and star fruit offer a wide range of nutrients. In addition to vitamin C, they provide many B vitamins, minerals such as potassium and dietary fibre.

Try pineapple or lychees in poultry salads, or sweet dates with bitter leaves. Bananas add a welcome freshness to winter salads of carrots and other root vegetables.

Dried fruits

Dried fruits – apricots, raisins and sultanas, cranberries and blueberries, prunes and so on – are rich in energy (calories) because their water content is lower than in their fresh counterpart and therefore the sugars are more concentrated. They are also a valuable source of fibre and of nutrients such as potassium and iron. Dried fruits are wonderfully versatile ingredients for both sweet and savoury salads.

Buying, storing and preparing fruit

- Buy fruit that is unbruised and that looks in good condition. If you want to keep it for more than 1–2 days, buy it almost ripe, rather than completely ripe.
- Wash fruit in cold water– don't leave it soaking – then pat dry.
- Prepare fruit as close to serving time as possible, because once cut it will start to lose vitamin C.
- To retain maximum nutrients, try to use fruit raw rather than cooked. Leave on the skin, prepare just before using and don't cut into very small pieces.

▲ Remove stones from cherries, using a stoner for neat results

► Use a zester to take very fine shreds from citrus fruit

► Score mango halves into cubes, press in the flesh side to pop them out and cut off the cubes with a knife

▼ Slip redcurrants from their stalks with the help of a fork

▲ Carefully spoon the seeds from pomegranate halves, discarding all the white pith

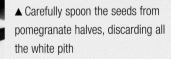

◄ Use kitchen scissors to snip dried apricots and other dried fruits into small pieces

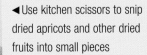

Salads with protein power

Adding protein-rich foods – meat, fish, eggs and cheese – to a salad turns it into a main dish, boosting the essential nutrients as well as the flavour. Because they are low in some vitamins and fibre, most protein-rich foods need to be served with others that contribute these elements – and salads are the perfect answer.

Hearty meat and poultry

Meat and poultry contain many nutrients and their protein content is high, so a little can go a long way in a salad. Red meat contains iron of the type that is most easily absorbed into the body. It is also rich in B vitamins, including B_{12} – not present in most plant foods – plus vitamin D and zinc. Poultry and game birds are another important source of B vitamins. They also provide many essential minerals such as zinc, iron, copper, selenium, phosphorus, potassium and magnesium.

When choosing meat for salads, look for the leanest cuts, and trim off any visible fat. Discard the skin from poultry before or after cooking, to keep fat levels low. The healthiest cooking methods for meat and poultry for salads are grilling or griddling, roasting, poaching and stir-frying.

Meat and poultry lend themselves to a wide variety of robust flavourings. Here are some salad ideas to try:
• Marinate steak in a mixture of soy sauce, fish sauce and chilli sauce, then griddle, slice and serve in a noodle and vegetable salad.
• Gently mix strips of leftover roast lamb or pork with warm boiled new potatoes and crunchy vegetables.
• Poach chicken fillets and cool, then slice and serve in a yogurt dressing with chopped apple or dried apricots, celery, almonds and crisp leaves.
• Stir-fry slices of chicken breast and mix while warm with raw bean sprouts, mange-tout and sliced mushrooms.
• Cut cooked turkey into chunks and mix with shredded cabbage, carrots, celery, raisins or sultanas, and toasted walnuts. Dress with a walnut oil vinaigrette.

A taste of the sea

Fish and shellfish are excellent low-fat protein foods that can add exciting textures and flavours to salads. White fish offers B-complex vitamins, and oil-rich fish, such as salmon and mackerel, are a major source of essential omega-3 fatty acids, which make a positive contribution to cardiovascular health. Shellfish such as prawns, crab, lobster, mussels, oysters and scallops supply many essential minerals, including selenium, calcium, phosphorus, iodine and iron.

Canned fish is ideal for quick salads. The canning process softens the bones in fish such as sardines and salmon and makes them palatable, and eating them boosts calcium intake.

◄ Griddle lean duck breast, slice and toss with radicchio, red chard and orange segments in an orange juice and ginger dressing

► Drain canned tuna and fold with canned cannellini beans and red onion in a herb vinaigrette

◀ Add sieved hard-boiled egg to watercress, spinach and cos lettuce and finish with a creamy yogurt dressing

▶ Scatter Parmesan shavings over a vinaigrette-dressed salad of sweet pear slices, rocket and frisée

Here are some ideas for delicious seafood salads.

• Cut 'meaty' white fish, such as swordfish and monkfish, into chunks and marinate in a mixture of lemon juice, extra virgin olive oil, garlic and chilli; then thread onto skewers with red peppers and grill. Mix the fish and peppers with green salad leaves and drizzle a spicy vinaigrette over them.

• Flake smoked mackerel or trout and fold into cooled cooked rice together with chopped cucumber, celery and spring onions, orange segments, chopped apple and red or purple grapes. Make the dressing with orange and lemon juices instead of vinegar.

• Mix strips of smoked salmon with chunks of cucumber and crisp salad hearts in a horseradish-flavoured creamy dressing.

• Poach fresh salmon fillet, then break into large flakes and toss while still warm into a hearty leaf salad with pieces of avocado and cherry tomatoes.

• Grill small scallops and sliced bulb fennel, then mix with red onion and rocket in a herb vinaigrette.

• Steep peeled cooked prawns in a mixture of lime juice and fresh coriander before tossing with grated carrot, lamb's lettuce, rocket and shredded iceberg lettuce.

• Spoon fresh white crab meat onto Little Gem lettuce leaves and yellow pepper, and dress with a herb vinaigrette.

Versatile eggs

Eggs are great for salads, either as a main ingredient or as a nutritious garnish. They provide useful amounts of vitamins A, B_2, B_{12}, E and niacin as well as iron.

• Halve hard-boiled eggs and pour over a creamy dressing flavoured with fresh dill or chives.

• Chop hard-boiled egg and scatter over a rice salad.

• Sieve hard-boiled egg into salad dressings.

• Poach eggs, then drain and arrange on baby spinach or frisée leaves. Garnish with crisp-fried strips of Parma ham.

Cheese variety

Adding cheese to a bowl of salad leaves and vegetables is a very easy way to make a main dish salad, and there are lots of different cheeses to choose from. Cheese is a valuable source of calcium, zinc, phosphorus, and vitamins B_2 and B_{12}.

• Try soft cheeses such as brie and camembert in a salad with celery, watercress and grapes.

• Grate or crumble hard cheeses like Cheddar and Stilton and add to a winter coleslaw.

• Spice up bland cottage cheese or fromage frais with red peppers, spring onions, fresh chives and other herbs, and fruits such as pineapple, mango or apricot.

• Grill slices of haloumi cheese and serve atop a bulghur wheat salad such as tabbouleh.

• Cut goat's cheese into thick discs, then grill and serve on a bed of salad leaves with a garnish of raspberries.

• Shave fresh Parmesan into long curls and scatter over a pasta salad or a warm salad of roast Mediterranean vegetables (aubergines, courgettes and peppers).

• Toss crumbled feta with chunks of apple, baby spinach leaves and toasted walnuts.

salad sensations

Pulses, grains, nuts and seeds

More of us are discovering the variety that can be brought to salads with the addition of pulses – beans, peas and lentils – grains such as rice, bulghur wheat, couscous and pasta, and nuts and seeds. Using protein from plant sources like pulses and nuts can make salads as nutritious as those containing meat.

Pulse power

Pulses offer an excellent balance of protein and carbohydrate, and are a very rich source of dietary fibre, particularly soluble fibre, which can help to lower blood cholesterol levels. Most are good sources of B-group vitamins and supply minerals such as iron and zinc.

Pulses are really useful in salads because they come in such a wide variety of different colours, shapes, sizes and textures. Most have a starchy, quite bland flavour that marries well with robust or intensely flavoured salad ingredients. Dried beans and peas have to be soaked and cooked before use (lentils do not need soaking), so for salads it's usually more convenient to use canned versions – they're just as nutritious.

● Combine lentils with roasted red peppers and garlic, or with poached salmon. Lentils are also delicious in potato salads.

● Make a Mexican-style salad with red kidney beans, onions, tomatoes, sweetcorn, chilli and cumin.

● Mix together butter, black-eyed and cannellini beans with celery, onions and a herb vinaigrette.

● Try pale green flageolet beans in a warm lamb salad.

● Use chickpeas in a Middle Eastern salad with tomatoes, onions and aubergines; a little feta will boost the protein content. Or purée chickpeas and thin with olive oil, to make a creamy dressing for a salad of roast Mediterranean vegetables.

The goodness of grains

Grains are an important source of starchy carbohydrate in salads, and they provide fibre – more if you choose wholegrains rather than refined versions – B vitamins and minerals. Grains also add interest and texture contrast.

Toss canned borlotti beans with mixed salad leaves, fresh herbs and sweet onion rings in a roasted garlic vinaigrette

Fold flaked smoked trout and peas into mixed long-grain and wild rice, and dress with a curry-spiced vinaigrette

- Cook wholewheat – whole berries of wheat – like rice, and add mixed dried fruit (apricots, prunes and sultanas) plus some toasted pecans or walnuts. Use fruit juice in the dressing and spice with cinnamon or ginger.
- Simmer kasha (buckwheat grains) until tender, then toss with sliced mushrooms, tiny broccoli florets, cherry tomatoes and a herb vinaigrette.
- Soak bulghur wheat, then add cucumber, tomatoes, garlic, fresh mint and lots of parsley to make tabbouleh. Or mix the soaked bulghur wheat with grated lemon zest and juice, cinnamon, chopped mint and parsley, and extra virgin olive oil, and spoon onto slices of avocado.
- Cover couscous with boiling water and let it swell, then fluff up and add diced carrots and celery with a mint and lemon dressing, or peppers, onions, sun-dried tomatoes, chickpeas and a chilli vinaigrette.
- Cook small pasta shapes until almost al dente, then cool under cold running water. Toss with a pesto dressing, and add seafood such as cooked peeled prawns or canned tuna, lots of crunchy salad vegetables and some fresh basil.
- Quickly rehydrate Oriental noodles, drain and flavour with soy sauce, toasted sesame oil and chilli. Add bean sprouts, watercress, and grated carrot and mooli.
- Don't forget about making salads with bread, which is one of the handiest sources of starchy carbohydrate. Use slightly stale bread, or bake or toast it until crisp. Pitta, ciabatta, French bread and rustic country-style breads all work well, in chunks or torn into pieces.

Nutritious nuts and seeds

Nuts and seeds bring crunchy texture to all kinds of salads, as well as providing vitamin E, iron, zinc, magnesium, protein and fibre. Some seeds, notably linseeds (sometimes called flax), also provide heart-healthy omega-3 fatty acids. Nuts and seeds are high in calories because of their fat content, but, with the exception of coconut, the saturated fat content is very low: nuts are high in monounsaturated fats, while seeds are high in polyunsaturated fats.

When buying nuts choose whole ones, but not those that are roasted and salted, as they are high in sodium and depleted of their essential fats. To enhance their flavour, nuts can be lightly toasted in a dry frying pan or under the grill.

Toast walnuts and mix with dessert apple and celery in a creamy dressing, to make a classic Waldorf salad

- Coarsely chop blanched or unblanched almonds and add to cheese, chicken and pasta salads.
- Very finely chop or grind brazil nuts and mix into salad dressings.
- Add whole cashew nuts to Oriental poultry salads and to winter root vegetable salads.
- Combine whole toasted hazelnuts with shredded carrots and white cabbage or use in a kasha salad.
- Garnish Thai-inspired salads with chopped peanuts.
- Add mild-flavoured pecan nuts to both sweet and savoury fruit salads.
- Toast pine nuts, toss with baby spinach leaves or other well-flavoured salad leaves and top with crumbled goat's cheese.
- Add toasted walnuts to a winter salad of rocket and sweet orange segments.
- Sprinkle linseeds over a rice or wholegrain salad.
- Include poppy seeds in a dressing for a savoury fruit salad, or use to garnish a cheese salad.
- Scatter toasted pumpkin seeds over a steamed pumpkin, rice and leek salad.
- Lightly toast sesame seeds and mix into Oriental salads. Include toasted sesame oil in the dressing.
- Add sunflower seeds to a salad of apple, citrus fruits, Cheddar cheese and dark leaves.

Herbs for salads

Fresh herbs can give a wonderful burst of flavour to a salad, and may bring extra nutritional benefits too.

Basil Traditional in a pesto dressing, basil's small leaves have a pungent and delicious flavour. Scatter over any tomato salad, but particularly one with mozzarella cheese.

Chervil A good winter herb, delicate and pretty chervil tastes slightly of aniseed and parsley. It goes well with carrots and other root vegetables.

Chives In common with other members of the onion family, the grass-like leaves of chives are rich in beneficial sulphur compounds and allicin, a phytochemical that helps to prevent heart disease. Snip chives over meat, poultry, fish or leaf salads.

Coriander Powerful, spicy-tasting coriander leaves are an essential ingredient in Oriental and Mexican-style salads. They are decorative too, with their round, frilled-edge petals.

Dill The mild caraway taste of feathery dill leaves works well in seafood, potato and cucumber salads.

Mint With its strong fresh flavour and good green colour, mint is one of the most popular herbs, and is delicious in potato and bean salads as well as with fruits such as melon and mango.

Oregano and marjoram These closely related herbs with very small leaves have a strong flavour, so use them sparingly in tomato salads or warm salads of courgette, aubergine or lamb. They are a traditional flavouring in a Greek salad.

Parsley The classic garnish for savoury dishes, parsley is also a tasty addition to a herb or leaf salad, particularly Italian or flat-leaf parsley. Parsley is a good source of folate, iron and vitamin C.

Purslane A herb from Greece and Turkey, purslane has fleshy, round, mid-green leaves with a mild, fresh flavour. Add a few leaves to a mixed leaf salad or scatter over a potato salad.

Rosemary One of the most aromatic of herbs, needle-like rosemary leaves are best used in warm vegetable, pork, lamb and fish salads.

Tarragon The lance-shaped leaves of this herb have a strong aniseed flavour that is perfect in chicken salads.

Thyme Tiny yet very aromatic, thyme leaves are good in potato and bean salads as well as in warm salads with beef and duck.

Clockwise from back left:
parsley, chives, oregano,
rosemary, basil, mint
and thyme

Dressed in style

A good dressing can make all the difference between a pleasant salad and an outstanding one, complementing and enhancing the salad ingredients, rather than overwhelming them. And salad dressings can add extra nutrients such as vitamins, calcium and healthy monounsaturated fats.

The right ingredients

Salads can be dressed simply with fresh fruit juice, or with a vinaigrette or creamy dressing. Vinaigrettes usually consist of an oil base sharpened with vinegar or an acidic fruit juice, plus seasoning and flavourings such as fresh herbs. Creamy dressings are based on mayonnaise, yogurt, fromage frais and so on. Most dressings can be whisked together with a fork, or, in the case of vinaigrette, shaken in a screw-top jar.

Oils

Good-quality oils contain beneficial phytochemicals, so it makes sense to use the best that you can afford. Extra virgin cold-pressed oils are the 'top of the range'. These are produced with minimal heat and refining processes, and thus retain more of their phytochemicals and essential fatty acids. Cheap blended vegetable oils that have been highly refined (the paler the colour, the more refined they are) have little goodness left in them. They may also contain oils high in saturated fat, such as coconut oil.

Choosing the right oil is vital to the success of a dressing. Olive oil is the classic for most vinaigrettes. Olive oil is like wine – different varieties of olive and a different growing region will give the oil its own special properties, and it can be peppery, salty, fruity, creamy and mild, and so on. Some olive oils are so delicious that they can be used alone to dress a salad. Have at least one basic mild extra virgin olive oil and then experiment with others.

Sunflower and groundnut oils are good for lighter salad dressings. Walnut and hazelnut oils work well with salads that include cheese, chicken, celery, spinach, apples and green beans, and can be mixed with olive or another oil to make them go further. Toasted sesame oil, often used in Oriental dressings, has a smoky, nutty flavour. You can also find oils flavoured with herbs and fresh chillies, and these can add extra zest to plain salads.

Keep oils in a cool, dark place to prevent them from oxidising and going rancid. Nut oils are particularly susceptible to oxidisation, so it is best to buy them in small quantities.

Vinegars

There are many vinegars you can use in salad dressings. The classic is wine vinegar (red or white, with red being slightly more robust in flavour). Sherry vinegar has an even fuller flavour. Richest of all the wine-based vinegars is balsamic, which should be used sparingly. It is so delicious it is often sprinkled over a salad on its own as a dressing. Fruit vinegars are made by steeping fresh fruit, such as raspberries, in white wine vinegar. Sharp and refreshing apple cider vinegar is good in dressings for cheese and ham salads. Rice vinegar, with its delicate flavour, is traditional in Oriental salad dressings.

Creamy dressings

Mayonnaise is the classic base for creamy dressings, but it is high in fat and calories. A healthier alternative can be made with yogurt or by mixing yogurt with mayonnaise. Yogurt (along with other dairy products) is a valuable source of calcium and contains beneficial bacteria that help to maintain a healthy digestive tract. Greek-style yogurt is deliciously rich; bio yogurt is mild and creamy; low-fat plain yogurt has a pleasant tangy flavour.

Other calcium-rich dairy products that make a good base for salad dressings are soured cream, crème fraîche and fromage frais. Even if they are higher in fat than low-fat yogurt, they are still a healthy alternative to mayonnaise. Reduced-fat versions of mayonnaise, Greek-style yogurt, soured cream, crème fraîche and fromage frais are also available, for an even lower fat creamy salad dressing.

Myriad flavourings

Ring the changes with vinaigrettes and creamy dressings by adding different seasonings and flavourings.

- Choose fresh herbs to complement the ingredients in the salad. Try thyme and rosemary for a roast Mediterranean vegetable salad, parsley and mint for a broad bean salad.
- Coarsely ground black pepper, with salt, is the classic seasoning for any dressing, but other spices can enliven a salad dressing too. Try paprika or cayenne pepper in a dressing for seafood and pasta salads; mustard or poppy seeds for leaf salads; caraway seeds in a creamy dressing for cabbage and root vegetable salads; ground cardamom and coriander for carrot, rice and grain salads. A little curry paste can be mixed into a dressing for a chicken salad.
- Use fresh flavourings such as lemongrass, garlic, chilli and ginger in Oriental salad dressings.
- Add a gentle bit of heat with Dijon mustard, a traditional component of a vinaigrette. Crunchy wholegrain mustard is also delicious.
- Roast a whole head of garlic until soft, then squeeze out the cloves, mash and mix into a creamy yogurt to make a healthy aioli dressing. Fresh garlic, finely chopped or crushed, is another dressing classic.
- Squeeze citrus juices for a tangy fresh flavour – try orange juice for a carrot salad, lime juice for a Thai salad or lemon juice for a Greek salad.
- Give a piquant touch to a dressing for seafood and poultry salads by adding capers.
- Sweeten soy-based Oriental salad dressings with honey or caster sugar.
- Finely chop black olives and mix into a vinaigrette for Mediterranean salads, or use tapenade (black olive paste).
- For seafood salads, flavour and colour a vinaigrette or creamy dressing with sun-dried tomato paste or ketchup.

Basic vinaigrette

A vinaigrette can be mixed specially for a salad or it can be made in a larger quantity, to use as required – it will keep in the fridge for several weeks. If made ahead, store it in a screw-top jar and shake well just before using.

Makes about 150 ml (5 fl oz)
120 ml (4 fl oz) extra virgin olive oil
2 tbsp red wine vinegar
1 tsp Dijon mustard or wholegrain mustard
pinch of caster sugar (optional)
salt and pepper

Preparation time: 2 minutes

Whisk all the ingredients together in a bowl, adding salt and pepper to taste. Alternatively, put all the ingredients in a screw-top jar, put on the lid and shake well.

Some more ideas

• For herb vinaigrette, add 1 tbsp chopped fresh herbs of your choice, such as tarragon, chives or thyme. If storing the vinaigrette, add the herbs just before using.
• For chilli vinaigrette, add 1–2 seeded and finely chopped fresh red chillies. Replace 1 tbsp of the olive oil with toasted sesame oil, if you like.
• For garlic vinaigrette, add 1–2 finely crushed garlic cloves. For a milder taste, roast 1 bulb of garlic, wrapped in foil, in a preheated 180°C (350°F, gas mark 4) oven for 40 minutes or until tender. Leave until cool, then squeeze out the soft garlic cloves and add to the oil, whisking well.
• For raspberry vinaigrette, replace the wine vinegar with raspberry vinegar. Use 4 tbsp each of olive oil and walnut oil.
• For poppy seed vinaigrette, replace the olive oil with sunflower or groundnut oil and add 1–2 tsp poppy seeds. Use lemon juice instead of vinegar or, for a richer, more robust flavour, use 1 tbsp each of balsamic vinegar and red wine vinegar.
• For an Oriental vinaigrette, replace the wine vinegar with rice vinegar and add 1 tbsp soy sauce. Sweeten with a few drops of clear honey instead of sugar.

Basic creamy dressing

Made with fromage frais or yogurt, this rich, smooth and refreshing dressing is lower in fat than traditional creamy dressings based on mayonnaise. It can be stored in the fridge for 1–2 days.

Makes about 150 ml (5 fl oz)
120 ml (4 fl oz) fromage frais or Greek-style yogurt
1 tbsp lemon juice
2 tsp white wine vinegar
pinch of caster sugar
salt

Preparation time: 2 minutes

1 Put all the ingredients into a bowl, adding salt to taste, and stir together until evenly blended. Taste and add more sugar, salt or lemon juice, if necessary.
2 Cover the bowl with cling film and keep the dressing in the fridge until ready to use.

Some more ideas

• For an even lower fat dressing, use 8%-fat fromage frais and half-fat Greek-style yogurt. The result will still be very creamy.
• Add 1–2 tsp creamed horseradish for beef and smoked mackerel salads.
• Add 1–2 tsp sun-dried tomato paste for seafood salads.
• Add 1 finely chopped shallot for pasta salads. Alternatively, add 1 crushed garlic clove or 1 tsp garlic purée.
• Add 1–2 tsp curry paste for chicken salads.
• Add 1 tbsp chopped fresh herbs, such as coriander, basil (for pasta salads), parsley, chives or tarragon (for chicken salads).
• To make a dip for crudités, add 1–2 tbsp grated Cheddar cheese or crumbled soft blue cheese, such as Roquefort or Dolcelatte.

Quick Salad Meals

On the table in 30 minutes or less

Salads make perfect fast meals, and almost anything you
fancy can quickly be turned into a main dish salad by
mixing it with salad leaves and vegetables, both raw and
cooked. Try juicy sweet peaches with cottage cheese and
crunchy summer vegetables, or a Mediterranean mix of
chickpeas, cucumber, tomatoes and feta cheese. Enjoy the
delicate flavour of smoked salmon with pasta bows and a
lively watercress dressing; a robust sardine salad made
with herby Italian bread, tomatoes and broad beans; or
Scandinavian-style cured herrings
with new potatoes, apples and
chicory. Or what about Caesar
salad with chicken, green beans
and baked anchovy croutons?

Peachy cottage cheese

This fresh-tasting salad combines luscious, sweet peaches and crisp green vegetables with a generous portion of creamy cottage cheese. It is quick and easy to put together, taking only a little longer to make than a sandwich. Serve with warmed sunflower seed, walnut or pumpkin bread for a well-balanced lunch.

Serves 4

250 g (8½ oz) frozen broad beans

170 g (6 oz) mange-tout, halved

100 g (3½ oz) rocket

45 g (1½ oz) lamb's lettuce

4 ripe peaches, stoned and thinly sliced

450 g (1 lb) cottage cheese

4 tbsp toasted flaked almonds

cayenne pepper

sprigs of fresh dill to garnish

Honey and dill dressing

2 tbsp extra virgin olive oil

grated zest and juice of 1 lemon

1 tsp wholegrain or Dijon mustard

2 tsp clear honey

2 tbsp chopped fresh dill

salt and pepper

Preparation time: about 30 minutes

Each serving provides ⓥ

kcal 338, protein 26 g, fat 17 g (of which saturated fat 4 g), carbohydrate 22 g (of which sugars 15 g), fibre 8 g

✓✓✓	A, B₁, B₂, C, E
✓✓	calcium, zinc
✓	iron

1 Plunge the broad beans into a saucepan of boiling water and cook for 4 minutes. Add the mange-tout and cook for 1 more minute. Drain the beans and mange-tout in a sieve, and refresh under cold running water.

2 To make the dressing, put the oil, lemon zest and juice, mustard, honey, chopped dill, and salt and pepper to taste in a mixing bowl. Whisk well.

3 Add the mange-tout, broad beans, rocket leaves and lamb's lettuce, and toss to coat with the dressing.

4 Divide the dressed vegetables among 4 serving plates. Scatter over the peach slices and top with the cottage cheese. Sprinkle with the flaked almonds and a little cayenne pepper. Garnish with dill sprigs and serve.

Some more ideas

• For a peachy fromage frais salad, omit the cottage cheese and the dressing, and instead mix together 340 g (12 oz) fromage frais, the juice of 1 lime, 1 crushed garlic clove and 3 tbsp chopped fresh coriander. Toss this with the vegetables, and top with the peaches.

• For a mango and ricotta salad, replace the peaches with 1 large mango, peeled, stoned and sliced, and use ricotta instead of cottage cheese. Blanch the mange-tout as in the main recipe and mix with 85 g (3 oz) watercress and 3 small heads of chicory, cut across into thick shreds. For the dressing, use the grated zest and juice of 2 limes instead of lemon, and 3 tbsp chopped fresh coriander instead of dill. Finish with 30 g (1 oz) roughly chopped toasted hazelnuts instead of almonds.

• To reduce the fat content, use low-fat cottage cheese. It contains 1.4 g of fat and 78 kcal per 100 g (3½ oz), whereas the same weight of standard cottage cheese contains 3.9 g of fat and 98 kcal.

• Use 4 hard-boiled eggs, cut into wedges, instead of the cottage cheese.

Plus points

• In addition to protein and calcium, cottage cheese provides useful amounts of vitamins B₂ and B₁₂.

• Broad beans, which were a staple peasant food in the Middle Ages, are high in soluble fibre, which helps to reduce blood cholesterol levels. Broad beans also contain protein and beta-carotene, plus some vitamin C, vitamin E, niacin and iron. A 100 g (3½ oz) portion will provide more than one-quarter of the daily requirement of phosphorus, which is needed for healthy bones and teeth.

• Fresh peaches are a good source of vitamin C and provide some beta-carotene.

Tabbouleh with goat's cheese

Tabbouleh is a classic Middle Eastern salad made with bulghur wheat. While the wheat is soaking, you have just enough time to chop the vegetables and herbs, and make the dressing. Serve with lavash or pitta bread.

Serves 4

280 g (10 oz) bulghur wheat

1 yellow pepper, seeded and chopped

20 cherry tomatoes, quartered

1 small red onion, finely chopped

10 cm (4 in) piece of cucumber, seeded and chopped

1 large carrot, grated

5 tbsp chopped parsley

2 tbsp chopped fresh coriander

2 tbsp chopped fresh mint

1 small fresh red chilli, seeded and finely chopped (optional)

200 g (7 oz) rindless soft goat's cheese, crumbled

salt and pepper

Lemon and cumin dressing

¼ tsp ground cumin

1 small garlic clove, very finely chopped

1 tbsp lemon juice

3 tbsp extra virgin olive oil

To serve

lettuce leaves

12 radishes, sliced

Preparation time: about 30 minutes

1 Put the bulghur wheat in a mixing bowl, pour over enough boiling water to cover and stir well. Leave to soak for 15–20 minutes.

2 Meanwhile, make the dressing. Whisk together the cumin, garlic and lemon juice in a small bowl, then whisk in the olive oil.

3 Drain the bulghur wheat in a sieve, pressing out excess water, then return it to the bowl. Add the pepper, tomatoes, onion, cucumber, carrot, parsley, coriander and mint, plus the chilli, if using. Pour the dressing over the top and season with salt and pepper to taste. Fold gently to mix well.

4 Arrange the lettuce leaves on 4 plates or a serving platter. Pile the bulghur salad on the leaves and sprinkle the goat's cheese over the top. Garnish with the radishes and serve.

Plus points

- Bulghur wheat is a good, low-fat source of starchy (complex) carbohydrate. Because it retains the particularly nutritious outer layers of the wheat grain, it contains useful amounts of B vitamins, particularly B_1.
- Goat's cheese is a tasty source of protein and calcium and lower in fat than cheeses such as Cheddar and Parmesan.

Some more ideas

- Use feta cheese instead of goat's cheese.
- For an apricot tabbouleh side salad, mix the soaked bulghur wheat with the yellow pepper and red onion, plus 4 chopped celery sticks and 115 g (4 oz) snipped, ready-to-eat dried apricots (omit the other vegetables and the herbs, as well as the goat's cheese). Add ½ tsp ground cinnamon to the dressing.
- For a spicy tabbouleh with chicken to serve 6, replace the goat's cheese with 2 cooked skinless boneless chicken breasts, about 280 g (10 oz) in total, cut into cubes. Mix the soaked bulghur wheat with the chicken, pepper, onion, carrot and parsley (omit the other vegetables and herbs). For the dressing, gently warm 3 tbsp extra virgin olive oil in a small frying pan with 1 finely chopped garlic clove. Add ½–1 tsp each of ground cumin, ground coriander, dry mustard and curry powder, and continue cooking for 1 minute. Stir in 2 tbsp lemon juice and seasoning to taste. Pour the dressing over the salad and stir gently to combine. Garnish with sliced cucumber rounds.

Each serving provides

kcal 473, **protein** 16 g, **fat** 18 g (of which saturated fat 7 g), **carbohydrate** 64 g (of which sugars 10 g), **fibre** 3 g

✓✓✓	B_1, B_6, B_{12}, E, niacin
✓✓	A, B_2, C, folate, calcium, copper, iron
✓	potassium

Smoked salmon with pasta bows

This colourful and nutritious salad is full of delicious textures and flavours. Little bows of pasta and peas are mixed with a creamy, fresh green dressing made from watercress and herbs, then garnished with more watercress and topped with pieces of smoked salmon. It makes a feast for the eyes.

Serves 4

250 g (8½ oz) farfalle (pasta bows)
100 g (3½ oz) shelled fresh or frozen peas
150 g (5½ oz) watercress
1 garlic clove
4 sprigs of parsley
2 sprigs of fresh tarragon
5 spring onions, chopped
4 tbsp plain low-fat yogurt
2 tbsp mayonnaise
½ red onion, chopped
2 tbsp capers, rinsed
¼ cucumber, diced
1 tbsp sunflower oil
1 tbsp white wine vinegar, or to taste
125 g (4½ oz) smoked salmon, cut into
   thin strips
salt and pepper

Preparation time: about 30 minutes

Each serving provides

kcal 379, protein 20 g, fat 12 g (of which saturated fat 2 g), carbohydrate 54 g (of which sugars 5 g), fibre 5 g

✓✓✓	B$_1$, B$_6$, C, E, niacin
✓✓	A, folate, copper, selenium, zinc
✓	B$_2$, calcium, iron, potassium

1 Cook the pasta in boiling water for 10–12 minutes, or according to the packet instructions, until al dente, adding the peas 2–3 minutes before the end of the cooking time. Drain in a sieve and rinse well with cold water, then drain again.

2 While the pasta and peas are cooking, put 50 g (1¾ oz) of the watercress in a food processor or blender and process until finely chopped. Add the peeled garlic clove, parsley, tarragon and half of the spring onions, and process to a fine purée. Add the yogurt and mayonnaise, and process briefly to combine. Stir in the remaining spring onions, and season with salt and pepper to taste.

3 Add the dressing to the cooked pasta and peas, and mix well together. Divide among 4 plates. Toss the remaining watercress with the red onion, capers, cucumber, oil and vinegar, and spoon over the pasta salad. Arrange the pieces of smoked salmon on top and serve.

Another idea

● Make a crab meat and rice noodle salad. Cut 85 g (3 oz) mange-tout and 1 small carrot into matchstick strips, and drop into a pan of boiling water with 1 thinly sliced courgette. Bring back to the boil, then remove from the heat. Add 250 g (8½ oz) thin rice noodles (ones that need no cooking) and leave to soak for 4 minutes. Drain, rinse with cold water and drain again. Toss the vegetables and noodles with 1 can crab meat, about 170 g, drained, 1 red pepper, seeded and thinly sliced, and 3 thinly sliced spring onions. Make a dressing with 2 tbsp toasted sesame oil, 1 tbsp rice vinegar, 1 tbsp dry sherry, 1 tbsp soy sauce, 1–2 chopped garlic cloves, 1 tbsp grated fresh root ginger and 1 tsp caster sugar. Serve on a bed of rocket, garnished with chopped fresh coriander.

Plus points

● Smoked salmon, like other oily fish, is a rich source of omega-3 fatty acids, which can help to protect against high blood pressure, heart disease and stroke. Omega-3 fatty acids also play a vital role in the development of eye and brain tissue, and studies suggest that there may be beneficial effects for the baby if mothers increase their intake of oily fish while they are pregnant and breast-feeding.

● Allicin, the compound that gives garlic its characteristic smell and taste, acts as an antibiotic and also has anti-fungal properties. Some allicin is destroyed in cooking, so for maximum benefit, eat garlic raw.

Chicken Caesar salad

A variation on the classic Caesar salad, this includes chunks of tender chicken, green beans and tasty anchovy croutons, all tossed in a light creamy dressing. Serve with warmed sesame seed French bread.

Serves 4

200 g (7 oz) thin green beans

1–2 cos lettuces, about 450 g (1 lb) in total, torn into bite-sized pieces

1 small head chicory, sliced crossways

4 celery sticks, sliced

400 g (14 oz) cooked skinless boneless chicken breasts (fillets), cut into chunks

1 egg

1 can anchovy fillets, about 50 g

1 garlic clove, crushed

12 thin slices of French bread, about 100 g (3½ oz) in total

30 g (1 oz) Parmesan cheese, finely pared into shavings or grated

Caesar dressing

1 tsp Dijon mustard

3 tbsp extra virgin olive oil

2 tsp sherry vinegar or wine vinegar

2 tbsp plain low-fat yogurt

large pinch of caster sugar

½ tsp Worcestershire sauce

pepper

Preparation time: about 30 minutes

1 Preheat the oven to 200°C (400°F, gas mark 6). Cook the beans in a saucepan of boiling water for 3 minutes or until just tender. Drain and refresh under cold running water. Halve the beans and put into a large salad bowl. Add the lettuce, chicory, celery and chicken. Set aside in the fridge.

2 Put the egg in a saucepan, cover with cold water and bring to the boil. Reduce the heat and simmer for 10 minutes.

3 Meanwhile, tip the anchovies into a bowl with the oil from the can (about 1 tbsp). Add the garlic and mash with a fork to a paste. Spread thinly over one side of each slice of French bread. Arrange on a baking sheet and bake for about 10 minutes or until the croutons are crisp and golden. Cool slightly, then break into pieces.

4 While the croutons are baking, make the Caesar dressing. Whisk together the mustard, olive oil, vinegar, yogurt, sugar, Worcestershire sauce and pepper to taste. Cool the hard-boiled egg under cold running water, then peel and chop. Stir into the dressing.

5 Drizzle half of the dressing over the chilled salad and toss to coat everything evenly. Add the croutons and toss again. Drizzle over the remaining dressing and scatter the Parmesan shavings on top. Serve at once.

Plus points

• Caesar salad is usually very high in fat, partly due to the quantity of oil in the dressing. In this healthier version, some of the oil is replaced by yogurt, to make a dressing that is just as delicious.

• Although celery contains very little in the way of vitamins, it does provide useful amounts of potassium as well as a phytochemical called phthalide, which may help to lower high blood pressure.

Each serving provides

kcal 382, **protein** 37 g, **fat** 23 g (of which saturated fat 4 g), **carbohydrate** 20 g (of which sugars 5 g), **fibre** 4 g

✓✓✓	B₁, B₆, B₁₂, E, niacin
✓✓	B₂, calcium, potassium, selenium, zinc
✓	iron

quick salad meals

38

Some more ideas

● For a lower fat dressing, use only 1½ tbsp olive oil and increase the yogurt to 4 tbsp.

● For a more traditional Caesar salad, to serve as a starter or side salad, mix 1 torn cos lettuce and 1 Little Gem lettuce, separated into leaves, in a large salad bowl. Cut 140 g (5 oz) day-old crusty white bread into 2 cm (¾ in) cubes. Put on a baking sheet and drizzle with 2 tbsp extra virgin olive oil, then bake as in the main recipe. To make the dressing, heat 2 tbsp extra virgin olive oil in a small pan and gently cook 3 peeled garlic cloves for 3 minutes. Add 1 can anchovy fillets, about 50 g, drained, and cook for a further 2–3 minutes or until the garlic is soft. Lift out the anchovies and garlic, reserving the oil, and mash to a paste. Mix in 1 tbsp Dijon mustard, 2 tsp balsamic vinegar and pepper to taste. Gradually whisk in the reserved oil, then stir in 2 tbsp plain low-fat yogurt. Drizzle half the dressing over the salad leaves and toss well to coat, then add the croutons and toss again. Drizzle over the remaining dressing and top with the shavings of Parmesan.

Focaccia and fennel with sardines

Based on the classic Tuscan bread salad *Panzanella*, this nutritious dish combines heart-healthy canned sardines with chunks of herby Italian bread moistened with fresh tomato juice. Crunchy fennel, broad beans, peppery rocket and capers add their flavours, complementing the fish perfectly.

Serves 4

170 g (6 oz) frozen broad beans

2 cans sardines in oil, about 120 g each, drained

3 tbsp extra virgin olive oil

2 tsp lemon juice

1 mild Spanish onion, halved and thinly sliced

2 tbsp drained capers

1 bulb of fennel

3 large or 4 medium-sized ripe beefsteak tomatoes, about 750 g (1 lb 10 oz) in total

1 herbed focaccia or ciabatta bread, about 280 g (10 oz), torn into 2.5 cm (1 in) pieces

100 g (3½ oz) rocket

Preparation time: about 30 minutes

Each serving provides

kcal 449, **protein** 25 g, **fat** 20 g (of which saturated fat 3 g), **carbohydrate** 43 g (of which sugars 11 g), **fibre** 8 g

✓✓✓	A, B$_1$, B$_6$, B$_{12}$, C, E, folate, niacin, calcium, selenium
✓✓	fibre, iron, potassium, zinc
✓	B$_2$

1 Cook the broad beans in boiling water for 5–6 minutes. Meanwhile, split each sardine in half lengthways. Drain the broad beans and refresh under cold running water. Set aside.

2 Put the oil and lemon juice in a salad bowl and whisk together. Stir in the onion slices and capers.

3 Trim any feathery fronds from the fennel and finely chop them. Cut the fennel bulb in half lengthways, then cut into thin slices. Add the slices and chopped fronds to the salad bowl and toss to coat with the dressing.

4 Cut the tomatoes into quarters. Scoop out the seeds and put them in a sieve held over a large mixing bowl. Press with the back of a spoon to extract the juice – you should have about 150 ml (5 fl oz). Discard the seeds. Cut the tomato quarters into thin wedges.

5 Add the bread to the mixing bowl and toss to moisten with the tomato juice. Tip the bread into the salad bowl. Add the sardines and broad beans, the tomato wedges and rocket. Toss gently to coat everything with the dressing, taking care not to break up the sardines too much. Serve immediately.

Some more ideas

● Canned salmon is an excellent alternative to sardines. Drain and flake the fish.

● If you can't find herbed focaccia or ciabatta, use a plain one and add 2 tbsp chopped fresh herbs such as basil or dill to the dressing.

● Instead of broad beans, use a can of flageolet beans, about 200 g. They need only to be drained and rinsed.

Plus points

● Try to eat oily fish, such as sardines, at least twice a week as they provide essential fatty acids that may help to reduce the risk of heart disease. The bones in canned sardines are softened and edible, and a useful source of calcium.

● Records show that onions have been cultivated since at least 3000BC, and throughout history they have been highly prized for their medicinal properties as well as for their flavour. In medieval times, they were hung in bunches on doors as protection against the plague. Onions are rich in a type of dietary fibre called fructoligosaccarides (FOS), which is believed to stimulate the growth of friendly bacteria in the gut while inhibiting the growth of harmful bacteria. Studies suggest that FOS also helps to protect against heart disease and cancer.

quick salad meals

Cajun-style ham and beans

This tempting salad combines smoky ham, red onion, sweetcorn, canned black-eyed beans and lots of fresh coriander in a spicy soured cream dressing. For generous, meaty chunks of ham, buy pieces from the deli counter rather than thin pre-packed slices. Serve with tomato wedges and crusty fresh bread.

Serves 4

2 cans black-eyed beans, about 410 g each, drained and rinsed

350 g (12½ oz) frozen sweetcorn, cooked and drained

3 celery sticks, sliced

1 small red onion, chopped

1 green pepper, seeded and diced

200 g (7 oz) piece of smoked ham, cut into 1 cm (½ in) chunks

sprigs of fresh coriander to garnish

Cajun dressing

150 ml (5 fl oz) soured cream

1 tbsp tomato ketchup

15 g (½ oz) fresh coriander, finely chopped

1½ tsp Cajun seasoning

Tabasco sauce

salt and pepper

Preparation time: about 25 minutes

1 To make the dressing, put the soured cream, ketchup, coriander, Cajun seasoning, 2 shakes of Tabasco sauce, and salt and pepper to taste in a large bowl. Whisk together, then taste and add more Tabasco if liked.

2 Add the beans, sweetcorn, celery, red onion, green pepper and ham to the bowl, and stir until everything is well mixed. Garnish with sprigs of coriander and serve at once.

Some more ideas

• If you cannot find Cajun seasoning, mix 1½ tsp paprika with ½ tsp cayenne pepper.

• Use a can of sweetcorn, about 340 g, drained and rinsed, instead of frozen sweetcorn.

• As an alternative to ham, try cooked gammon or roast chicken or turkey.

• Make a quick tandoori chicken and chickpea salad. For the dressing, mix 150 g (5½ oz) plain low-fat bio yogurt with 1 tbsp extra virgin olive oil, 15 g (½ oz) fresh coriander, finely chopped, 1 tsp toasted cumin seeds, the juice of 1 lemon, a shake of Tabasco sauce and seasoning to taste. Drain and rinse 1 can of chickpeas, about 410 g, and 1 can of red kidney beans, about 410 g, and add to the dressing together with 1 small red onion, finely chopped, ½ diced cucumber and 200 g (7 oz) shredded green spring cabbage. Cut 250 g (8½ oz) boneless tandoori chicken into cubes, and fold into the salad. Serve with naan bread.

Plus points

• Black-eyed beans are a good low-fat source of protein and, in common with all other beans, they are a good source of dietary fibre, particularly soluble fibre. This can help to reduce high blood cholesterol levels, thereby lessening the risk of heart disease. Beans and other pulses also provide useful amounts of vitamin B_1.

• The canning process has little effect on the nutritional value of pulses, so canned beans are a nutritious ingredient to have on hand in the storecupboard. Rinsing the beans thoroughly will help to reduce some of the sugars that can cause flatulence.

• Sweetcorn offers vitamins A (from beta-carotene), C and folate as well as dietary fibre. Although the vitamins are lost in canned sweetcorn, they are retained in the frozen vegetable.

Each serving provides

kcal 419, protein 33 g, fat 12 g (of which saturated fat 6 g), carbohydrate 48 g (of which sugars 9 g), fibre 10 g

✓✓✓	B_1, B_6, C, E, folate, niacin, zinc
✓✓	A, B_2, iron, potassium
✓	calcium, selenium

quick salad meals

Chicken liver and raspberry salad

The fruity fresh flavour of juicy raspberries and a splash of raspberry vinegar balance the richness of chicken livers in this easy warm salad, which is a popular lunch dish in French bistros. Cooking the livers in a non-stick pan means the minimum of oil is needed. Serve with French country bread.

Serves 4

400 g (14 oz) chicken livers

150 g (5½ oz) mixed lettuce leaves, such as Oak Leaf, romaine and Lollo Rosso

100 g (3½ oz) baby spinach leaves

4 tbsp chopped fresh flat-leaf parsley

4 tbsp snipped fresh chives

3 tbsp extra virgin olive oil

100 g (3½ oz) shallots, finely chopped

1 large garlic clove, crushed

3 tbsp raspberry vinegar

125 g (4½ oz) raspberries

salt and pepper

Preparation and cooking time: about 20 minutes

1 Trim the chicken livers, removing any cores and green bits. Cut any large pieces in half. Pat dry with kitchen paper and set aside.

2 Arrange the lettuce and spinach leaves on a platter. Sprinkle with the parsley and chives. Set aside.

3 Heat 2 tbsp of the olive oil in a large non-stick frying pan. Add the shallots and garlic and fry over a low heat for about 3 minutes or until softened, stirring occasionally.

4 Increase the heat to moderate and add the remaining 1 tbsp oil to the pan. Add the chicken livers and fry, stirring occasionally, for 5 minutes or until they are cooked through – remove one piece and cut it open; it should be light pink in the centre.

5 Turn the heat to high, add the raspberry vinegar and stir. Season with salt and pepper to taste. Pour the hot liver mixture over the salad, scatter on the raspberries and serve at once.

Some more ideas

● Red wine vinegar can be used instead of raspberry vinegar.

● Instead of raspberries and raspberry vinegar, use fresh blueberries and blueberry vinegar. The flavours work well with chicken livers. Blueberry vinegar is available from speciality food shops and delicatessens.

● For a chicken liver and sultana salad, poach the livers rather than frying them. Put them in a saucepan with 1 chopped carrot, 1 chopped celery stick and a bay leaf. Cover with water and bring to the boil, skimming the surface as necessary. Reduce the heat and simmer for about 5 minutes or until the livers are cooked through but still pink in the centre. Meanwhile, whisk 4 tbsp extra virgin olive oil, 2 tbsp balsamic vinegar and seasoning to taste in a salad bowl. Add the lettuce and spinach leaves and toss to coat with the dressing. Drain the chicken livers well (discard the vegetables and bay leaf) and add to the salad bowl together with 4 tbsp sultanas or raisins. Toss again, then sprinkle with chopped parsley and serve.

Plus point

● According to a recent survey carried out by the Department of Health, 1 in 3 British women under the age of 50 has low iron levels, which can lead to tiredness and increased susceptibility to colds and infections. Chicken livers are an excellent source of iron, with 100 g (3½ oz) cooked chicken livers providing over half of the recommended daily intake. They are also an excellent source of several of the B vitamins, vitamin A, zinc and copper.

Each serving provides

kcal 196, **protein** 20 g, **fat** 11 g (of which saturated fat 2 g), **carbohydrate** 4 g (of which sugars 3 g), **fibre** 2 g

✓✓✓	A, B₁, B₂, B₆, B₁₂, C, E, folate, niacin, copper, iron, selenium, zinc
✓✓	potassium

quick salad meals

45

Heringsalat

Horseradish, caraway and dill flavour this tasty Danish-style salad of pickled herrings, apples and new potatoes on a bed of bitter leaves. The dressing is based on low-fat yogurt, mixed with a little mayonnaise for added creaminess. Enjoy the salad for a fast midweek supper.

Serves 4

800 g (1¾ lb) new potatoes, scrubbed and thickly sliced

2 red-skinned dessert apples

4 tsp lemon juice

115 g (4 oz) radishes, sliced

115 g (4 oz) radicchio, separated into leaves

2 heads of chicory, separated into leaves

50 g (1¾ oz) walnut pieces

400 g (14 oz) sweet cured herrings in dill marinade, drained and cut into pieces

salt and pepper

Horseradish and caraway dressing

150 g (5½ oz) plain low-fat yogurt

2 tbsp mayonnaise

2 tsp creamed horseradish

1 tsp clear honey

½ tsp caraway seeds

To garnish

¼ tsp caraway seeds

1 tbsp chopped fresh dill

Preparation time: about 30 minutes

Each serving provides

kcal 552, **protein** 25 g, **fat** 27 g (of which saturated fat 2 g), **carbohydrate** 55 g (of which sugars 25 g), **fibre** 4 g

✓✓✓	A, B₁, B₆, C, folate, niacin
✓✓	B₂, potassium
✓	calcium, iron, zinc

1 Cook the potatoes in a saucepan of boiling water for 5 minutes or until just tender. Drain, rinse with cold water and drain again.

2 To make the dressing, mix together the yogurt, mayonnaise, creamed horseradish, honey and caraway seeds in a large mixing bowl. Season with salt and pepper to taste. Add the potatoes and stir to coat them with the dressing.

3 Quarter, core and dice the apples. Toss them in the lemon juice, then add to the potatoes together with the radishes. Fold in gently.

4 Divide the radicchio and chicory leaves among 4 individual serving plates and sprinkle with the walnut pieces. Spoon the potato salad over the leaves, and arrange the herring on top. Garnish with caraway seeds and chopped dill, and serve.

Some more ideas

• Instead of the horseradish dressing, use the horseradish-flavoured variation of Basic creamy dressing (see page 29).

• Make a smoked mackerel and potato salad. Use 3 sliced ripe plums instead of the apples (omit the lemon juice), and 1 finely chopped red pepper instead of radishes. Serve on radicchio leaves (omit the chicory and walnuts) and top with 400 g (14 oz) smoked mackerel fillet, skinned and flaked into pieces.

• For an Indian-style chicken and potato salad, use 400 g (14 oz) cooked skinless boneless chicken breasts (fillets), cut into strips, instead of the cured herrings. Flavour the dressing with 2 tsp mild curry paste instead of horseradish, honey and caraway seeds. With the cooked potatoes, add 1 peeled, stoned and diced mango, 2 sliced celery sticks and 4 finely chopped spring onions (omit the apples, radishes and walnuts). Spoon onto a bed of green salad leaves and top with the chicken.

Plus points

• Herring is an excellent source of vitamin D and provides useful amounts of vitamin A and potassium. These nutrients are retained in pickled herring.

• Apples contain the simple sugar fructose, which is metabolised by the body slowly, so helping to control blood sugar levels.

• Leaving the skins on potatoes and apples adds fibre to the diet, which keeps the digestive tract healthy. It also preserves nutrients found just under the skin.

Feta and chickpea salad

Made from ewe's milk, Greek feta cheese has a good tangy, slightly salty flavour. Cow's milk feta produced in other countries has a milder taste. Either type can be used in this classic Mediterranean salad, with ripe tomatoes, olives, cucumber and chickpeas. Serve with pitta bread warmed under the grill.

Serves 4

2 Little Gem lettuces, separated into leaves

4 ripe tomatoes, chopped

1 green pepper, seeded and cut into 1 cm (½ in) squares

1 small red onion, thinly sliced

1 cucumber, cut into quarters lengthways and then into chunks

1 can chickpeas, about 410 g, drained and rinsed

60 g (2¼ oz) stoned black olives, preferably Greek Kalamata olives

150 g (5½ oz) feta cheese, cut into small cubes

Parsley and mustard dressing

3 tbsp extra virgin olive oil

1½ tbsp lemon juice

1 tsp Dijon mustard

3 tbsp chopped fresh flat-leaf parsley

pepper

Preparation time: about 20 minutes

Each serving provides Ⓥ

kcal 347, **protein** 16 g, **fat** 21 g (of which saturated fat 7 g), **carbohydrate** 24 g (of which sugars 8 g), **fibre** 8 g

✓✓✓	A, B₁, B₆, C, E, niacin
✓✓	B₁₂, folate, calcium, iron, potassium
✓	copper, zinc

1 Put all the dressing ingredients into a large salad bowl, adding pepper to taste (there is no need to add salt as the cheese is salty). Whisk together.

2 Add the lettuce leaves, tomatoes, green pepper, onion, cucumber, chickpeas and olives, and toss gently to combine and coat everything with the dressing.

3 Scatter the cubes of feta cheese over the salad, toss again gently and serve immediately.

Another idea

- Make a Middle Eastern-style goat's cheese and lentil salad. Cook 250 g (8½ oz) Puy lentils in boiling water for about 25 minutes, or according to the packet instructions, until tender. Drain thoroughly and leave to cool slightly, then add 6 tbsp Basic vinaigrette (see page 29) flavoured with ½ tsp ground cumin and 2 tbsp chopped fresh coriander. Toss well. Add 1 sliced red onion, 4 chopped plum tomatoes and 1 large grated carrot, and toss again until well mixed. Spoon onto Little Gem lettuce leaves in a salad bowl, and crumble over 150 g (5½ oz) goat's cheese.

Plus points

- Believing chickpeas to be a powerful aphrodisiac, the Romans fed them to their stallions to improve their performance. Although this reputation seems to be long forgotten, chickpeas do contribute valuable amounts of soluble fibre, iron, folate, vitamin E and manganese to the diet.

- The vitamin C from the lemon juice in the dressing will help to increase absorption of iron from the chickpeas.

- Although feta cheese is high in saturated fat and salt, it has a strong flavour so a little goes a long way.

Warm Salads

New ideas for tempting hot-and-cold dishes

A warm salad is a tantalising taste sensation – the delicious contrast of freshly poached seafood, griddled meat or poultry, or grilled vegetables served hot on a bed of crisp salad leaves or mixed into cool grains or noodles. There are lots of imaginative combinations here, such as juicy grilled chicken breasts with mango, new potatoes and a fresh orange dressing, or pan-fried asparagus and Parma ham with baby spinach leaves and crunchy croutons. Chunks of swordfish steak folded into a vitamin-packed tomato and pepper salsa, or strips of steak with Japanese buckwheat noodles and shiitake mushrooms are two other exciting ideas for warm salads.

Bulghur wheat salad with lamb

For this tasty dish, tender lamb fillet is quickly cooked under the grill, then cut up and mixed into a salad of bulghur wheat, red pepper, green olives and fresh mint. No oil is used to dress the salad, just fresh lemon and orange juices, so the fat content is kept healthily low.

Serves 4

200 g (7 oz) bulghur wheat

400 g (14 oz) lamb neck fillet, trimmed of fat and cut in half lengthways

4 shallots, finely chopped

1 large red pepper, seeded and chopped

100 g (3½ oz) stoned green olives

½ cucumber, chopped

4 tbsp chopped fresh mint

juice of 1 lemon

grated zest and juice of 1 orange

2 Little Gem lettuces, sliced across into shreds

salt and pepper

Preparation and cooking time: about 40 minutes

Each serving provides

kcal 395, protein 27 g, fat 12 g (of which saturated fat 4 g), carbohydrate 45 g (of which sugars 6 g), fibre 3 g

✓✓✓	A, B₁, B₆, B₁₂, C, E, niacin, zinc
✓✓	B₂, copper, folate, iron
✓	potassium

1 Preheat the grill. Put the bulghur wheat in a mixing bowl, pour over enough boiling water to cover and stir well. Leave to soak for 15–20 minutes.

2 Meanwhile, place the lamb on the grill rack and grill for 6–7 minutes on each side or until browned on the outside but still slightly pink inside. Remove from the heat and leave to rest in a warm place for 5–10 minutes, then slice into chunky pieces.

3 Put the shallots, red pepper, olives, cucumber and chopped mint in a salad bowl.

4 Drain the bulghur wheat in a sieve, pressing out excess water. Add to the salad bowl together with the lemon and orange juices, the orange zest, and salt and pepper to taste. Toss to mix everything well.

5 Add the lamb and lettuce, and toss again. Serve immediately.

Some more ideas

● Griddle the lamb instead of grilling it. Cut it in half lengthways and brush on both sides with extra virgin olive oil. Lay the slices in a hot ridged cast-iron grill pan and cook for about 5 minutes on each side.

● Make a spicy pork and bulghur wheat salad with pineapple. Preheat the oven to 220°C (425°F, gas mark 7). Mix together the grated zest of ½ orange, the juice of 1 orange, 1 tbsp dark rum or soy sauce, 1 tbsp sunflower oil, 2 tbsp muscovado sugar, 1 large crushed garlic clove, and ½ tsp each ground cinnamon, ground allspice and pepper in a shallow ovenproof dish. Add 400 g (14 oz) pork fillet (tenderloin) and turn to coat with the mixture. Roast for 25 minutes or until tender but still moist. Meanwhile, soak the bulghur wheat as in the main recipe, then mix with ½ sweet ripe pineapple, peeled, cored and chopped, 1 large red pepper, seeded and chopped, 4 shallots, thinly sliced, the juice of 1 orange, 55 g (2 oz) watercress sprigs and 1 tbsp chopped fresh coriander. Season to taste. Spoon onto 4 plates. Slice the pork and arrange on top of the salad. Spoon over the cooking juices and serve immediately while still warm.

Plus points

● Lamb is an excellent source of zinc, which is necessary for healing wounds. Lamb also provides useful amounts of iron.

● The olive, which is native to the eastern Mediterranean region, has been cultivated since at least 3000BC – it was taken to the New World in the 15th century by the Spanish. Olives contain about 18% fat by weight, and most of this is healthy monounsaturated fat.

Spinach, ham and asparagus salad

Here, pan-fried pieces of asparagus and Parma ham are combined with wilted baby spinach leaves and crisp baked croutons in a delicious warm salad for 2. Serve with a side dish of new potatoes tossed with a little extra virgin olive oil, snipped chives and black pepper, or with crusty French bread.

Serves 2

55 g (2 oz) crustless dark rye bread, cut into
    cubes
2 tbsp extra virgin olive oil
250 g (8½ oz) asparagus spears, cut into
    short pieces
2 garlic cloves, thinly sliced
4 shallots, cut into wedges
85 g (3 oz) Parma ham, trimmed of fat and
    torn into pieces
1 tbsp balsamic vinegar
2 tbsp lemon juice
1 tsp clear honey
250 g (8½ oz) baby spinach leaves
few shavings of Parmesan cheese, about
    15 g (½ oz) in total
salt and pepper

Preparation and cooking time: about 40 minutes

Each serving provides

kcal 372, protein 26 g, fat 21 g (of which saturated fat 5 g), carbohydrate 21 g (of which sugars 8 g), fibre 9 g

✓✓✓ A, B$_1$, B$_6$, C, E, folate, niacin

✓✓ B$_2$, calcium, iron, potassium, zinc

1 Preheat the oven to 200°C (400°F, gas mark 6). Toss the bread cubes with 1 tbsp of the olive oil, then spread out on a baking sheet. Bake for about 5 minutes or until crisp.

2 Meanwhile, heat the remaining 1 tbsp oil in a large wok or frying pan. Add the asparagus, arranging it in a single layer, and cook over a moderate heat for 5 minutes, without stirring. Turn the asparagus over, add the garlic and shallots, and cook for a further 3 minutes. Add the Parma ham and cook for 2 more minutes, stirring constantly.

3 Using a slotted spoon, remove the asparagus, ham and shallot mixture from the wok and put it in a bowl. Keep warm. Add the balsamic vinegar, lemon juice and honey to the wok, and stir to mix with the cooking juices. Add the spinach and cook, stirring and turning, until just wilted.

4 Season the spinach with salt and pepper to taste, then divide between 2 plates. Arrange the asparagus, ham and shallot mixture on top. Spoon on any cooking juices and scatter over the croutons and shavings of Parmesan. Serve immediately.

Some more ideas

● Make a spinach and pear salad with Camembert, to serve 2. Heat 1 tbsp extra virgin olive oil in a non-stick frying pan, and fry 4 chopped shallots with 15 g (½ oz) pecan nuts until the nuts are lightly toasted. Meanwhile, divide 125 g (4½ oz) baby spinach leaves between 2 shallow bowls, and add 1 large avocado and 1 pear, both cut into slices lengthways. Add 1 tbsp balsamic vinegar, 1 tbsp lemon juice and 1 tsp clear honey to the shallots and nuts, and stir to mix, then add 115 g (4 oz) diced Camembert. Let it heat gently until starting to melt, then spoon the mixture over the salad and serve.

● Instead of Parma ham, use 4 rashers of lean smoked back bacon, rinded and cut into pieces. Add it with the asparagus.

Plus point

● Contrary to popular belief, spinach is not a particularly good source of iron, but it does have a lot of other nutrients to offer. It is a good source of several antioxidants, including vitamin C and vitamin E, and it provides useful amounts of the B vitamins folate, niacin and B$_6$. In addition, it offers several cancer-fighting phytochemicals.

Sesame pork and noodle salad

With its typical Chinese flavours – ginger, sesame, soy sauce and rice vinegar – this salad makes a delectable lunch or supper dish. It is very nutritious as most of the vegetables are raw. For the best effect, cut the pepper, carrot and spring onions about the same thickness as the noodles.

Serves 4

400 g (14 oz) pork fillet (tenderloin)
2 tsp grated fresh root ginger
1 large garlic clove, finely chopped
1½ tsp toasted sesame oil
3 tbsp light soy sauce
2 tbsp dry sherry
2 tsp rice vinegar
225 g (8 oz) fine Chinese egg noodles
1 red pepper, seeded and cut into matchstick strips
1 large carrot, cut into matchstick strips
6 spring onions, cut into matchstick strips
250 g (8½ oz) bean sprouts
150 g (5½ oz) mange-tout
2 tbsp sesame seeds
1 tbsp sunflower oil

Preparation and cooking time: 45 minutes

Each serving provides

kcal 454, protein 33 g, fat 13 g (of which saturated fat 3 g), carbohydrate 51 g (of which sugars 9 g), fibre 5 g

✓✓✓	A, B₁, B₆, B₁₂, C, E, niacin
✓✓	B₂, folate, copper, iron, zinc
✓	potassium, selenium

1 Trim all visible fat from the pork fillet. Cut the pork across into slices about 5 cm (2 in) thick, then cut each slice into thin strips.

2 Combine the ginger, garlic, sesame oil, soy sauce, sherry and vinegar in a bowl. Add the pork strips and toss to coat, then leave to marinate while you prepare the other ingredients.

3 Put the noodles in a large mixing bowl and pour over enough boiling water to cover generously. Leave to soak for about 4 minutes, or according to the packet instructions, until tender. Drain well and tip back into the bowl. Add the red pepper, carrot, spring onions and bean sprouts.

4 Drop the mange-tout into a pan of boiling water and cook for about 1 minute or until just tender but still crisp. Drain and refresh under cold running water. Add the mange-tout to the noodle and vegetable mixture and toss to mix. Set aside.

5 Toast the sesame seeds in a large frying pan over a moderate heat for 1–2 minutes or until golden, stirring constantly. Tip the seeds onto a piece of kitchen paper. Heat the sunflower oil in the frying pan, increase the heat slightly and add the pork with its marinade. Stir-fry for 4–5 minutes or until the pork is no longer pink.

6 Add the strips of pork and any cooking juices to the noodle and vegetable mixture, and stir gently to combine. Divide among 4 shallow bowls, sprinkle with the toasted sesame seeds and serve.

Plus points

• In the past, pork has had a reputation for being rather fatty, but this is certainly no longer the case. Over the last 20 years, in response to consumer demands, farmers have been breeding leaner pigs. Pork now contains considerably less fat, and it also contains higher levels of the 'good' polyunsaturated fats. The average fat content of lean pork is less than 3%, much the same as that contained in skinless chicken breast.
• The vegetables in this dish provide a good variety of different nutrients, in particular vitamin C and beta-carotene.

Another idea
● For a sesame pork and rice noodle salad, use 250 g (8½ oz) rice noodles instead of egg noodles. Soak them as in the main recipe, then mix with the red pepper, carrot and spring onions (omit the bean sprouts and mange-tout).

Cut off the leaves from 200 g (7 oz) small pak choy and reserve; cut the stalks across into 1 cm (½ in) thick slices. Drain the marinade from the pork and reserve. Heat 1 tbsp extra virgin olive oil in a frying pan and stir-fry the pork with 125 g (4½ oz) baby corn, cut in half

lengthways, for 1½ minutes. Add the pak choy leaves and stalks, and stir-fry for 1 minute or until the leaves just begin to wilt and the pork is cooked. Tip into the bowl with the noodles and vegetables. Heat the reserved marinade in the frying pan, pour it over the salad and toss well.

Puy lentil and sausage salad

Tiny green Puy lentils have a slightly nutty texture and flavour, and are perfect in salads as they keep their shape well once cooked. Here they are mixed with grilled venison sausages and Mediterranean vegetables, plus a handful of fresh rocket leaves. All you need to accompany the dish is some crusty French bread.

Serves 6

300 g (10½ oz) Puy lentils

2 red peppers, halved and seeded

4 courgettes, halved lengthways

3 tbsp extra virgin olive oil

450 g (1 lb) high-meat-content venison
   sausages

2 small white or red onions, cut into wedges

2 celery sticks, thinly sliced

2 garlic cloves, thinly sliced

300 g (10½ oz) new potatoes, scrubbed and
   cut into dice

2 tbsp chopped fresh thyme

4 tbsp chopped fresh flat-leaf parsley

2 tbsp sherry vinegar

1 tbsp German or Dijon mustard

45 g (1½ oz) rocket

Preparation and cooking time: about 1 hour

Each serving provides

kcal 544, protein 36 g, fat 26 g (of which
saturated fat 7 g), carbohydrate 45 g (of
which sugars 11 g), fibre 8 g

✓✓✓	A, B$_1$, B$_6$, C, E, folate, niacin, copper, iron, selenium
✓✓	potassium, zinc
✓	B$_2$

1 Preheat the grill. Rinse the lentils and put them in a large saucepan of water. Bring to the boil, then reduce the heat, cover and simmer gently for about 25 minutes or until just tender. Drain, reserving a little of the cooking water.

2 While the lentils are cooking, rub the skins of the red peppers and courgettes with a little of the oil. Arrange the vegetables, skin side up, in the grill pan, in one layer. Add the sausages. Grill for 10–15 minutes, turning the sausages occasionally, until they are cooked and browned on all sides and the vegetables are tender. Transfer the peppers to a polythene bag and leave until cool enough to handle, then peel off the skins.

3 Heat the remaining oil in a large frying pan and add the onions, celery, garlic and potatoes. Stir-fry for about 10 minutes or until tender.

4 Roughly chop the sausages and the grilled peppers and courgettes, then add them to the frying pan. Also add the cooked lentils, thyme, parsley, vinegar and mustard. Stir well, and add a little of the lentil cooking water to moisten the mixture slightly. Season with salt and pepper to taste.

5 Transfer to a serving bowl and serve warm or cool. Toss in the rocket leaves just before serving.

Some more ideas

• For a quick version of this salad, replace the dried lentils with 2 cans lentils, about 300 g each, drained and rinsed. Slice the sausages and chop all the vegetables, including the peppers and courgettes. Stir-fry them all together for 10 minutes or until the sausages are cooked. Add the lentils with the other ingredients in step 4.

• To make a chickpea, rice and chorizo salad, cook 300 g (10½ oz) Camargue red rice for 30–35 minutes or until tender; drain and cool. Heat 2 tbsp extra virgin olive oil in a frying pan, and stir-fry 2 chopped red peppers, 2 sliced red onions and 140 g (5 oz) thinly sliced chorizo for 4–5 minutes or until the vegetables start to soften. Add to the rice, with 1 can chickpeas, about 400 g, drained and rinsed, 300 g (10½ oz) halved cherry tomatoes, 25 g (scant 1 oz) shredded fresh basil leaves, 2 tbsp balsamic vinegar and seasoning to taste.

Plus points

• Venison is very low in fat compared to other red meat, and provides excellent amounts of iron and B vitamins.

• Puy lentils are an excellent source of fibre, particularly the soluble variety. They also provide useful amounts of many B vitamins, particularly B$_1$ and B$_6$, and of iron.

warm salads

58

Mango chicken salad

Here is a very special salad – new potatoes, slices of tender grilled chicken and asparagus tossed in a mellow fresh orange dressing while still warm and then gently mixed with juicy mango slices and baby salad leaves. It makes a delicious and well-balanced meal all on its own.

Serves 4

1 garlic clove, crushed

1 tsp grated fresh root ginger

1 tbsp light soy sauce

2 tsp sunflower oil

2 skinless boneless chicken breasts (fillets), about 170 g (6 oz) each

800 g (1¾ lb) new potatoes, scrubbed

2 large sprigs of fresh mint

125 g (4½ oz) asparagus spears

1 ripe mango, peeled and sliced

150 g (5½ oz) mixed baby salad leaves, such as spinach, red chard, and cos and Lollo Rosso lettuces

Fresh orange dressing

½ tsp finely grated orange zest

1 tbsp orange juice

1 tsp Dijon mustard

2 tbsp sunflower oil

1 tbsp walnut oil

salt and pepper

Preparation and cooking time: 50 minutes, plus 15 minutes marinating

Each serving provides

kcal 361, **protein** 24 g, **fat** 13 g (of which saturated fat 2 g), **carbohydrate** 40 g (of which sugars 9 g), **fibre** 4 g

✓✓✓	B_1, B_6, C, E, folate, niacin
✓✓	A, potassium, zinc
✓	B_2, iron

1 Put the garlic, ginger, soy sauce and sunflower oil in a bowl and whisk together. Add the chicken breasts and turn to coat both sides, then leave to marinate for 15 minutes.

2 Put the potatoes in a saucepan, pour over boiling water to cover and add the mint sprigs. Cook for 15–20 minutes or until tender. At the same time, put the asparagus in a steamer basket or metal colander, cover and set over the pan of potatoes to steam. Cook thin spears for 4–5 minutes, thick spears 8–10 minutes, or until just tender. Drain the potatoes (discard the mint) and leave until cool enough to handle, then cut into thick slices. Cut the asparagus diagonally into 6 cm (2½ in) lengths.

3 Preheat the grill to moderate. Remove the chicken from the marinade and place it on the grill rack. Grill for about 15 minutes, brushing frequently with the marinade and turning once, until cooked through and the juices run clear when the chicken is pierced with the tip of a knife. Leave to rest for 3–4 minutes, then slice.

4 To make the dressing, put the orange zest and juice, mustard and sunflower and walnut oils in a large serving bowl, and whisk together until slightly thickened. Season with salt and pepper to taste.

5 Transfer the warm sliced chicken, potatoes and asparagus to the serving bowl and gently toss together to coat with the dressing. Add the mango and salad leaves and toss gently again. Serve immediately, while still warm.

Plus points

● Mango is an excellent source of vitamin C and beta-carotene, both antioxidants that help to protect against damage by free radicals. Due to the beta-carotene content, mango is also one of the best fruit sources of vitamin A, providing more than 50% of the daily needs in half a large fruit.

● Chicken is an excellent source of protein, and by removing the skin, the fat content is kept low. It also contains B vitamins.

● Although potatoes contain much less vitamin C than fruit and other vegetables, they are an important source of this vitamin in the diet because they are eaten in such large quantities.

Some more ideas

- To save time, buy cooked or smoked chicken breasts. Remove the skin and slice.
- For a sharper citrus dressing, use lime zest and juice instead of orange.
- Make a turkey salad with fresh blueberries. Use turkey breast fillets, and marinate and grill as for the chicken in the main recipe. Cut 900 g (2 lb) new potatoes into 2 cm (¾ in) dice and cook in boiling salted water for 10 minutes or until just tender. Drain well and toss with the warm turkey slices in the fresh orange dressing. Put 150 g (5½ oz) blueberries in a small pan with 1 tbsp balsamic vinegar and 2 tsp clear honey. Gently bubble for 3–4 minutes or until the blueberries are tender. Add the salad leaves to the turkey and potato mixture and gently toss together, then drizzle over the warm blueberries.

Seafood with watercress dressing

Scallops and strips of salmon fillet are briefly poached in a little wine and stock, then lifted onto a colourful crunchy salad. The poaching liquid provides the base for a creamy dressing. Serve with crusty bread.

Serves 4

300 g (10½ oz) piece of skinless salmon fillet, cut into 4 strips

200 g (7 oz) small scallops without coral

3 tbsp dry white wine

200 ml (7 fl oz) fish stock

thin slice of fresh root ginger (there is no need to peel it)

225 g (8 oz) sugarsnap peas

140 g (5 oz) radishes

150 g (5½ oz) mixed salad leaves, including baby spinach, watercress, and cos and Oak Leaf lettuces

Watercress dressing

85 g (3 oz) watercress

1 shallot, chopped

thin strip of lemon zest

2 tbsp snipped fresh chives

1 tsp lemon juice

2 tbsp crème fraîche

salt and pepper

Preparation and cooking time: about 40 minutes

Each serving provides

kcal 231, **protein** 30 g, **fat** 13 g (of which saturated fat 2 g), **carbohydrate** 6 g (of which sugars 4 g), **fibre** 2 g

---

✓✓✓	A, B₁, B₆, B₁₂, C, E, niacin, selenium
✓✓	B₂, folate, potassium, zinc
✓	calcium, iron

1 Put the strips of salmon into a non-aluminium saucepan or sauté pan with a well-fitting lid – the pan should be just big enough for the salmon to fit in one layer. Arrange the scallops on top of the salmon. Pour over the wine and fish stock, and add the slice of ginger. Bring to the boil over a moderate heat, then lower the heat until the liquid is simmering very gently. Cover and poach for 5–8 minutes or until the salmon and scallops are cooked and feel just firm to the touch.

2 While the seafood is cooking, drop the sugarsnap peas into a pan of boiling water and cook for 3–4 minutes or until just tender but still crunchy. Drain, then refresh under cold running water. Set aside.

3 To make radish flowers, cut 5 slits round each radish, cutting down from the top almost to the base. Put into a bowl of iced water and leave until the 'petals' open slightly. Alternatively, simply slice the radishes.

4 Put the mixed leaves into a salad bowl. Add the sugarsnap peas and the drained radishes and mix well.

5 With a draining spoon, lift the seafood out of the pan onto a plate. Reserve the poaching liquid. Cut each strip of salmon in half, or flake into large chunks. Arrange the salmon and scallops on top of the salad.

6 To make the dressing, remove the tough stalks from the watercress and reserve. Drop the leaves into a pan of boiling water and bring back to the boil. Immediately drain and refresh under cold running water. Squeeze out excess water, then chop very finely.

7 Put the reserved watercress stalks in a pan with the shallot, lemon zest and 120 ml (4 fl oz) of the seafood poaching liquid. Half cover the pan and simmer for 5 minutes. Strain the liquid, discarding the zest and vegetables. Stir in the chopped watercress, chives, lemon juice and crème fraîche, and season with salt and pepper to taste. Spoon the warm dressing over the salad and serve.

Plus points

- Scallops are an excellent source of selenium, a powerful antioxidant that protects the body against disease, and of vitamin B₁₂. They also provide useful amounts of phosphorus and potassium.
- Watercress is a positive powerhouse of disease-fighting nutrients. It contains phytochemicals that help to protect against cancer and help to neutralise the damaging effects of smoking. It is also an excellent source of vitamin C and beta-carotene.

Another idea

● Try a warm smoked haddock and prawn salad. Poach 340 g (12 oz) smoked haddock fillet in the same way as the salmon, but omitting the ginger – the exact cooking time will depend on the thickness of the fish. Add

150 g (5½ oz) cooked peeled prawns (thawed if frozen) for the last 1–2 minutes, just long enough to heat them through. Remove the seafood, reserving the poaching liquid. Flake the haddock into large chunks, discarding the skin and any bones. For the salad, instead of

sugarsnap peas, radishes and mixed leaves, use 100 g (3½ oz) watercress or rocket, 2 small heads of radicchio, roughly torn, and 100 g (3½ oz) grated raw celeriac. Make a more piquant watercress dressing by adding ½–1 tsp creamed horseradish.

Marinated duck and kasha salad

Kasha, or buckwheat grain, is available either plain or roasted. When plain kasha is toasted and then simmered in stock, it develops a rich nutty flavour. It works perfectly with duck in this hearty main-dish salad.

Serves 4

450 g (1 lb) boneless duck breasts

2 garlic cloves, chopped

juice of 1 lemon

12 sprigs of fresh thyme

1 tsp chopped fresh rosemary

3 tbsp extra virgin olive oil

225 g (8 oz) plain kasha (buckwheat grain)

750 ml (1¼ pints) chicken stock

125 g (4½ oz) thin green beans

200 g (7 oz) mixed salad leaves, such as
  frisée, lamb's lettuce, mizuna and rocket

5 sprigs of fresh basil, finely shredded

½ red onion, thinly sliced

8 green olives, stoned

8 black olives, stoned

2 medium-sized courgettes, thinly sliced
  lengthways

12 small spring onions

12 small tomatoes

1½ tbsp red wine vinegar, or a combination
  of sherry and balsamic vinegars

salt and pepper

Preparation and cooking time: 50 minutes

Each serving provides

kcal 483, **protein** 30 g, **fat** 18 g (of which saturated fat 4 g), **carbohydrate** 55 g (of which sugars 6 g), **fibre** 5 g

✓✓✓ B$_1$, B$_2$, B$_6$, B$_{12}$, C, E, folate, niacin,
    copper, zinc

✓✓ A, iron, potassium

1 Remove all the fat and skin from the duck breasts. With a sharp knife, score the flesh on both sides in a criss-cross pattern. Put the breasts in a bowl and add about two-thirds of the garlic, the lemon juice, half of the thyme sprigs, the rosemary and 1 tbsp of the oil. Turn to coat the breasts with the flavourings, then marinate while you prepare the rest of the ingredients.

2 Put the kasha in a heavy frying pan and toast over a moderate heat, stirring and tossing, for 4–5 minutes or until it has become slightly darker in colour. Remove from the heat.

3 Bring the stock to the boil in a saucepan, then stir in the toasted kasha. Bring back to the boil. Reduce the heat, cover and cook over a low heat for 10–15 minutes or until the stock has been absorbed and the kasha is tender. Remove from the heat and set aside, still covered, until ready to use.

4 Heat a ridged cast-iron grill pan for 10 minutes. Meanwhile, drop the green beans into a saucepan of boiling water and blanch for 1–2 minutes. Drain and refresh under cold running water. Cut the beans in half and put into a salad bowl. Add the salad leaves, basil, red onion and olives, and toss to mix.

5 Remove the duck breasts from the marinade and place on the hot grill pan. Cook for 3 minutes, then turn the breasts over and cook for another 3 minutes (the meat will be rare, so cook longer if you prefer it well done). Remove the duck to a board. Place the courgettes, whole spring onions and whole tomatoes on the grill pan and cook for 1–2 minutes or until lightly charred all over.

6 Combine the remaining garlic and 2 tbsp oil with the vinegar in a small bowl, and add the leaves from the remaining thyme sprigs. Whisk together, then drizzle over the salad. Spoon on the kasha, and arrange the hot griddled courgettes, spring onions and tomatoes on top. Slice the duck breasts, place over the vegetables and serve.

Plus points

● Removing the skin and all visible fat from duck lowers the fat content substantially. Skinless duck breast contains only a fraction more fat than skinless chicken breast. Duck meat is rich in the minerals iron and zinc and also provides B vitamins.

● Despite its name, buckwheat is not a true grain, but a plant that produces cereal-like seeds. It is gluten-free, so it is suitable for anyone with gluten intolerance. It contains a phytochemical called rutin, which is believed to help reduce high blood pressure.

Another idea

● For a duck, kasha and pumpkin salad, rub the duck breasts with a mixture of 2 chopped garlic cloves, ½ tsp ground cumin, ¼ tsp ground cinnamon and ½ tsp cocoa powder, and put in a mixing bowl. Add 150 g (5½ oz) peeled and seeded pumpkin or butternut squash, thinly sliced, and sprinkle over the juice of 1 lemon, the juice of 1 orange and 1 tbsp extra virgin olive oil. Turn the ingredients to mix them, then leave to marinate for at least 30 minutes. Make the green bean and leaf salad and sprinkle with 75 g (2½ oz) dried cherries or fresh blackberries and 1 orange, peeled and segmented. For the dressing, whisk the juice of 1 orange with 2 tbsp extra virgin olive oil, 2 tsp caster sugar and ¼ tsp paprika. Griddle the duck breasts as in the main recipe, then slice. Griddle the pumpkin for 4–5 minutes. Pour the dressing over the salad, add the kasha and arrange the duck and pumpkin slices on top.

Melted brie with vegetables

In this unusual salad, a wonderfully creamy dressing, made simply from melted brie cheese delicately flavoured with tarragon, is spooned over spicy roasted potato wedges, baby plum tomatoes, green beans and red onion. It seems a very indulgent dish, but is a deliciously healthy main meal.

Serves 4

100 g (3½ oz) thin green beans, halved

900 g (2 lb) baking potatoes, scrubbed and cut into big wedges

1½ tbsp extra virgin olive oil

1 tsp paprika

1 tsp salt flakes

few coarsely crushed black peppercorns

2 tbsp sesame seeds

1 small iceberg lettuce, torn into bite-sized pieces

1 red onion, thinly sliced

½ cucumber, chopped

225 g (8 oz) baby plum or cherry tomatoes, halved

juice of 1 lemon

salt and pepper

Brie dressing

250 g (8½ oz) brie, rind removed and diced

4 tbsp semi-skimmed milk

1 tbsp finely chopped fresh tarragon

Preparation and cooking time: about 1 hour

Each serving provides Ⓥ

kcal 491, **protein** 21 g, **fat** 26 g (of which saturated fat 9 g), **carbohydrate** 48 g (of which sugars 8 g), **fibre** 6 g

✓✓✓	A, B₁, B₆, B₁₂, C, E, folate, niacin, calcium
✓✓	B₂, potassium, zinc
✓	iron

1 Preheat the oven to 200°C (400°F, gas mark 6). Heat a roasting tin in the oven. Drop the beans into a large saucepan of boiling water and blanch for 2 minutes. Using a draining spoon, scoop the beans out of the pan into a colander, and refresh under cold running water. Add the potatoes to the saucepan of boiling water and cook for 3 minutes, then drain.

2 Put the potato wedges in a bowl. Add the oil, paprika, salt flakes and crushed peppercorns, and toss to coat the potatoes. Tip them into the hot roasting tin. Roast for about 15 minutes. Sprinkle with the sesame seeds and roast for a further 30 minutes, turning once or twice, until crisp and browned.

3 When the potatoes are ready, remove from the oven and keep hot. Put the beans, lettuce, onion, cucumber and tomatoes in a mixing bowl. Add the lemon juice and salt and pepper to taste, and toss well.

4 To make the dressing, put the brie and milk into a saucepan and heat gently, stirring, until melted and well blended. Stir in the tarragon and a little pepper, and cook for a few seconds.

5 Spoon the bean and tomato salad into 4 bowls. Top with the roasted potatoes and spoon over the warm brie dressing. Serve at once.

Some more ideas

• Other cheeses can be made into a warm dressing in the same way. Try Camembert, Pie d'Angloys and Le Brin, or blue brie, Bleu de Bresse and Danish blue.

• Instead of making a dressing, simply top the hot roasted potatoes with the diced brie, which will melt with the heat from the potatoes.

• For very low-fat roast potatoes, use a can of spray olive oil. It is only 1 kcal per spray.

• For a fondue-style dressing, grate 170 g (6 oz) Gruyère cheese and put into a saucepan with 1 crushed garlic clove and 90 ml (3 fl oz) dry white wine. Mix 1 tsp cornflour with 2 tsp water and add to the pan. Bring to the boil, stirring constantly until melted and smooth. Drizzle over the salad and roasted potatoes.

Plus point

• Although brie is thought of as a high-fat, high-calorie cheese, it does not contain as much fat, weight for weight, as a hard, well-matured cheese such as Cheddar. This is because, with age, a cheese becomes drier and its overall bulk decreases, thus increasing the levels of fat by weight.

Lamb and wholewheat salad

Wholewheat – whole unprocessed wheat kernels or berries – has a deliciously chewy texture and nutty flavour, similar to brown rice. It makes an excellent base for this highly nutritious salad of quickly grilled lamb steak, sprouted mung beans, tomatoes and black olives in a vinaigrette dressing.

Serves 4

180 g (6½ oz) wholewheat

2 garlic cloves

400 g (14 oz) lean lamb leg steaks, trimmed of fat

1 tbsp extra virgin olive oil

250 g (8½ oz) sprouted mung beans, rinsed and drained

170 g (6 oz) cherry tomatoes, halved

2 celery sticks, thinly sliced

55 g (2 oz) rocket

85 g (3 oz) black olives, preferably Kalamata, stoned

5 tbsp Basic vinaigrette (see page 29)

pepper

Preparation and cooking time: about 1½ hours, plus 3 hours soaking

Each serving provides

kcal 573, protein 32 g, fat 29 g (of which saturated fat 7 g), carbohydrate 50 g (of which sugars 5 g), fibre 8 g

✓✓✓	B$_1$, B$_6$, B$_{12}$, E, folate, niacin, selenium, zinc
✓✓	B$_2$, C, iron, potassium
✓	A

1 Put the wholewheat in a bowl, cover with cold water and leave to soak for 3 hours.

2 Drain and rinse the wholewheat, then put into a saucepan with 1 peeled garlic clove and enough water to cover. Bring to the boil, then reduce the heat and simmer for about 1 hour or until tender. Drain thoroughly and leave to cool. Discard the garlic.

3 Preheat the grill to moderate. Place the lamb steaks on the grill rack. Crush the remaining garlic clove and mix with the oil and a little pepper. Brush the garlic-flavoured oil over the lamb, then grill for 4 minutes on each side or until cooked but still slightly pink in the centre. Remove from the heat and leave to rest on a carving board for 10 minutes.

4 Meanwhile, mix together the sprouted mung beans, tomatoes, celery, rocket and olives in a salad bowl. Add the wholewheat and spoon over the vinaigrette. Toss well together. Carve the lamb into thick slices and arrange on top. Serve at once.

Some more ideas

• Sprouted mung beans, available in cartons from healthfood shops, have been sprouted from high quality beans and have a larger bean and smaller sprouting part than conventional bean sprouts. This makes them more crunchy. If you cannot find them, you can use ordinary bean sprouts.

• Use long-grain brown rice instead of wholewheat. There is no need to soak it, and it will need about 30 minutes simmering.

• For a vegetarian wholewheat salad, omit the lamb and add 500 g (1 lb 2 oz) tiny new potatoes, steamed or boiled until tender and then left until just warm, and 1 large grated carrot. Instead of olives and tomatoes, use 75 g (2½ oz) toasted cashews and 2 tbsp each toasted sunflower and sesame seeds. Fold everything together with the wholewheat.

Plus points

• Lamb is an excellent source of vitamin B$_{12}$, needed for a healthy nervous system, and a good source of vitamin B$_1$.

• Sprouted beans are low in calories and extremely nutritious – they are a good source of vitamin C and folate as well as several phytochemicals, including lutein, coumarins and xanthophyll.

• In ancient Greece, celery was used to stimulate digestion and to eliminate excess fluids from the body – it is a natural diuretic. It also contains potassium.

Swordfish with salsa dressing

Orange juice adds a refreshing note to the salsa-style tomato and pepper dressing for this vibrant-looking salad. As the dressing can be made well in advance and the swordfish steaks take only minutes to cook, this is a very quick dish to prepare, ideal when you are entertaining. Serve with lots of sesame breadsticks or crusty bread.

Serves 4

4 swordfish steaks, about 1 cm (½ in) thick, 140 g (5 oz) each

1½ tsp extra virgin olive oil

250 g (8½ oz) baby spinach leaves

2 courgettes, coarsely grated

1 tbsp chopped parsley

Tomato salsa dressing

1 large orange

600 g (1 lb 5 oz) ripe tomatoes, seeded and cut into 5 mm (¼ in) dice

4 large spring onions, green parts only, finely chopped

1 orange pepper, seeded and cut into 5 mm (¼ in) dice

1 yellow pepper, seeded and cut into 5 mm (¼ in) dice

1 tsp ground cumin, or to taste

2 tbsp extra virgin olive oil

1 fresh green chilli, seeded and finely chopped

salt and pepper

2 tbsp finely chopped fresh coriander

Preparation and cooking time: 30 minutes, plus at least 20 minutes marinating

1 Prepare the salsa dressing at least 20 minutes (or up to 8 hours) before serving. Finely grate the zest from the orange and squeeze out 4 tbsp juice. Put the zest and juice in a large mixing bowl and add the tomatoes, spring onions, peppers, cumin, olive oil and chilli. Season with salt and pepper to taste. Stir, then cover and chill.

2 Preheat the grill to high. Lightly brush the swordfish steaks with some of the olive oil and place on the grill rack. Grill, about 7.5 cm (3 in) from the heat, for 2½ minutes. Turn the swordfish steaks over, brush with the rest of the olive oil and grill for a further 2½–3 minutes or until the edges are lightly charred and the flesh is just firm. Don't overcook or the swordfish will be tough and dry. Remove from the heat and set aside to cool slightly.

3 Meanwhile, put the spinach leaves, courgettes and parsley in a bowl and toss to mix. Divide among 4 plates.

4 Stir the coriander into the dressing. Break the swordfish into bite-sized pieces, add to the dressing and gently mix in, taking care not to break up the fish. Spoon the dressed fish on top of the spinach salad and serve.

Plus points

● Swordfish is a good low-fat source of protein and it is very nutritious, providing excellent amounts of vitamin B_{12}, niacin and selenium as well as useful quantities of potassium.

● Peppers are native to tropical America and have been cultivated in Europe since the 16th century. All peppers are a rich source of many important nutrients – they are a good source of beta-carotene and, weight for weight, they contain over twice as much vitamin C as oranges.

● Courgettes provide the B vitamins B_6, folate and niacin. The greatest concentration of these nutrients is found in the skin, which is also rich in the antioxidant beta-carotene.

Each serving provides

kcal 306, **protein** 31 g, **fat** 14 g (of which saturated fat 2 g), **carbohydrate** 16 g (of which sugars 15 g), **fibre** 6 g

✓✓✓	A, B_1, B_6, B_{12}, C, E, folate, niacin, selenium
✓✓	B_2, calcium, iron, potassium

Some more ideas

● Skinless salmon fillet can be substituted for the swordfish. Marlin (a type of shark) is another meaty fish alternative.

● Make a warm Mediterranean tuna salad, using 4 tuna steaks, 2 cm (¾ in) thick, about 140 g (5 oz) each. Grill the steaks, basting with a mixture of 1½ tsp extra virgin olive oil and 1 tbsp orange juice, for 2–3½ minutes on each side, according to how well done you like tuna. Instead of using the tomatoes in the salsa dressing, slice them. Make the salsa dressing omitting the cumin, chilli and coriander, and toss with 200 g (7 oz) shredded radicchio and 100 g (3½ oz) rocket. Arrange the tomato slices and salsa salad on 4 plates, top with the tuna, broken into pieces, and scatter over some shredded fresh basil.

Seared sirloin steak with soba

Strips of richly flavoured sirloin steak and shiitake mushrooms sit atop a bed of slightly wilted mixed salad leaves, with a mound of warm soba (buckwheat noodles) and a soy, ginger and sesame dressing.

Serves 4

1 garlic clove, chopped

4½ tsp soy sauce

1 tsp groundnut oil

2 thick-cut lean sirloin steaks, about 450 g (1 lb) in total, trimmed of fat

2 tsp grated fresh root ginger

1 tbsp caster sugar

3 tbsp rice vinegar or cider vinegar

2 tbsp toasted sesame oil

250 g (8½ oz) soba (Japanese buckwheat noodles)

200 g (7 oz) sugarsnap peas

115 g (4 oz) shiitake mushrooms, stalks removed

200 g (7 oz) mixed salad leaves, including frisée, mizuna, baby sorrel, baby spinach and coriander leaves

7.5 cm (3 in) piece of mooli (Japanese white radish), cut into matchstick strips

5 spring onions, thinly sliced

10 sprigs of fresh basil, leaves torn

Preparation and cooking time: 40 minutes

Each serving provides

kcal 490, **protein** 33 g, **fat** 15 g (of which saturated fat 3 g), **carbohydrate** 56 g (of which sugars 9 g), **fibre** 3 g

✓✓✓	B₁, B₆, B₁₂, C, niacin, copper, zinc
✓✓	B₂, E, iron, selenium
✓	folate

1 Mix together the garlic, 1 tsp of the soy sauce and the groundnut oil. Rub into both sides of the steaks and leave to marinate for a few minutes.

2 Meanwhile, put the remaining 3½ tsp soy sauce, the ginger, sugar, vinegar and sesame oil in a small bowl and whisk together for the dressing.

3 Cook the soba in a large pan of boiling water for 5 minutes, or according to the packet instructions, adding the sugarsnap peas for the last 2 minutes of the cooking time. Drain the noodles and peas.

4 Heat a ridged cast-iron grill pan. Add the steaks and cook over a high heat for 2½ minutes. Turn them over and cook for 1 minute. Add the shiitake mushrooms to the pan, cup side down. Cook for a further 1½–2 minutes. The steaks will be rare, so cook longer if you prefer them medium or well done. Remove the steaks to a board and cut into thin slices.

5 Place the mixed leaves in a large bowl and add the sugarsnap peas, mooli, spring onions and basil. Stir the dressing, then pour about two-thirds over the salad and toss. Add the rest of the dressing to the noodles and mix.

6 Arrange the leafy salad on a serving platter or on 4 plates and top with the soba, mushrooms and steak slices. Serve at once.

Plus points

• Red meat such as beef is a nutritious protein-rich food. Beef is an excellent source of zinc and a useful source of iron, and it provides B vitamins and vitamin D.

• Shiitake mushrooms contain a compound called lentinan, which is believed to help strengthen the immune system. The mushrooms are also thought to help protect against cancer by preventing normal cells from developing into tumours and by inhibiting tumour growth.

• Ginger is a natural remedy for travel sickness and morning sickness. Astronauts at NASA use ginger to prevent motion sickness because, unlike conventional anti-nausea medicines, it doesn't cause drowsiness. It is also believed to aid digestion and help the body fight off colds.

Some more ideas

• If mooli is not available, use red radishes cut into thin slices – their bright colour is very pleasing in the salad.

• If you cannot find soba, you can use any Chinese or Asian noodle, such as cellophane noodles or medium egg noodles.

• For an Italian steak and pasta salad, rub the steaks with a mixture of 1 chopped garlic clove, ½ tsp mixed dried Italian herbs and 1½ tsp extra virgin olive oil. For the dressing, mix

together 5 finely chopped plum tomatoes,
1 chopped garlic clove, 2 tbsp red wine vinegar,
a handful of fresh basil leaves, coarsely
chopped, 2 tbsp tomato purée, 2 tbsp extra
virgin olive oil and ½ tsp caster sugar. Instead
of soba, use 250 g (8½ oz) penne or other

pasta shapes, cooking them for 10–12 minutes,
or according to the packet instructions, until al
dente; drain (omit the sugarsnap peas). Toss the
salad leaves with half of the tomato-basil
dressing and arrange on a platter or 4 serving
plates. Scatter 1 small courgette, cut into

matchstick strips, and 1 red pepper, thinly
sliced, around the edge. Toss the hot pasta with
most of the remaining dressing and spoon it
into the middle of the salad. Thinly slice the
grilled steak, arrange on the pasta and spoon
on the rest of the dressing.

Middle Eastern lentil salad

This is a deliciously healthy and filling salad. The lentils are cooked with garlic and lemon plus a pinch of cumin, then dressed while warm. Mixed peppers and broccoli florets add colour, and the salad is finished with dried apricots, goat's cheese and toasted sunflower seeds. Serve with toasted pitta bread.

Serves 4

250 g (8½ oz) green lentils, rinsed

1 garlic clove

good pinch of ground cumin

1 slice of lemon

1 small red onion, finely chopped

85 g (3 oz) ready-to-eat dried apricots, roughly chopped

3 small peppers (1 red, 1 yellow and 1 green), seeded and cut into 2 cm (¾ in) squares

100 g (3½ oz) broccoli, broken into small florets

50 g (1¾ oz) firm rindless goat's cheese

2 tbsp toasted sunflower seeds

Lemon and coriander dressing

juice of 1 lemon

3 tbsp extra virgin olive oil

2 tbsp finely chopped fresh coriander

salt and pepper

Preparation and cooking time: about 50 minutes

Each serving provides Ⓥ

kcal 400, **protein** 22 g, **fat** 16 g (of which saturated fat 3 g), **carbohydrate** 45 g (of which sugars 14 g), **fibre** 10 g

✓✓✓ B$_1$, B$_6$, C, E, folate, niacin, iron, selenium

✓✓ A, B$_2$, potassium, zinc

✓ B$_{12}$, calcium

1 Put the lentils in a large saucepan, cover with water and bring to the boil, skimming off any scum. Add the peeled garlic, cumin and lemon, then reduce the heat and simmer for about 30 minutes or until the lentils are tender.

2 Meanwhile, to make the dressing, put the lemon juice, oil, coriander, and salt and pepper to taste into a large salad bowl, and whisk together.

3 Drain the lentils, discarding the lemon and garlic, and add them to the salad bowl. Toss gently to mix with the dressing.

4 Add the onion, apricots, peppers and broccoli florets, and mix gently. Crumble the cheese over the top, scatter over the sunflower seeds and serve immediately.

Some more ideas

• Instead of goat's cheese, top the salad with 4 sliced hard-boiled eggs.

• Use 150 g (5½ oz) frozen broad beans instead of broccoli florets. Cook the beans in boiling water for 5 minutes or until tender. Drain, then refresh under cold running water.

Plus points

• Like all pulses, lentils are a good source of soluble fibre, which can help to reduce high blood cholesterol levels. Lentils also offer protein, starchy carbohydrate and B vitamins.

• Dried apricots are an excellent source of beta-carotene and a useful source of calcium.

• The sunflower was first brought to Europe around 1510 as a decorative plant and it wasn't until the 18th century that sunflowers began to be grown as a crop for the production of sunflower oil. Sunflower seeds are rich in healthy polyunsaturated fats and they are a good source of the antioxidant vitamin E, which helps to protect cell membranes from damage by free radicals and vitamin B$_1$. They also provide useful amounts of the minerals zinc, iron, copper, phosphorus, selenium and magnesium.

Haloumi cheese with aubergines

Haloumi, a firm-textured Greek ewe's milk cheese, tastes wonderful grilled until tinged golden brown (eat it warm as it toughens on cooling). Its salty flavour goes particularly well with aubergine slices, cooked until crisp on the outside and soft inside, then tossed in a sweet-sharp herb dressing with polenta croutons.

Serves 4

3 tbsp extra virgin olive oil

1 strip of lemon zest

1 small sprig of fresh thyme

1 small sprig of fresh rosemary

675 g (1½ lb) small aubergines, cut into
1 cm (½ in) slices

1 tbsp balsamic vinegar

1 tsp lemon juice

1 tbsp plain flour

250 g (8½ oz) haloumi cheese, cut into 2 cm
(¾ in) cubes

1 romaine or cos lettuce, torn into large
pieces

250 g (8½ oz) baby plum or cherry tomatoes,
halved

30 g (1 oz) stoned green olives

salt and pepper

fine shreds of lemon zest to garnish

Polenta croutons

750 ml (1¼ pints) hot vegetable stock or
water

170 g (6 oz) instant polenta

2 tbsp chopped fresh flat-leaf parsley

pinch of freshly grated nutmeg

Preparation and cooking time: 50 minutes, plus
1 hour infusing and cooling

1 Put the olive oil in a small saucepan with the lemon zest, thyme and rosemary. Gently heat for 2–3 minutes, lightly bruising the herbs with the back of a spoon to release their flavour, until the herbs begin to sizzle. Remove from the heat and leave to infuse for 1 hour.

2 Meanwhile, cook the polenta for the croutons. Pour the stock or water into a saucepan and bring to the boil. Gradually add the polenta, stirring constantly. Cook for 5–10 minutes, or according to the packet instructions, until thick. Stir in the parsley and season with the nutmeg, and salt and pepper to taste. Pour the polenta into a greased 18 x 28 cm (7 x 11 in) shallow tin and spread out evenly. Leave to cool for about 1 hour, then turn out onto a board and cut into 1 cm (½ in) cubes.

3 Preheat the grill to moderately hot. Lightly score a criss-cross pattern on one side of each aubergine slice. Strain the flavoured oil through a sieve into a jug and whisk in the balsamic vinegar and lemon juice.

4 Lightly brush both sides of the aubergine slices with the oil mixture and arrange on the rack in the grill pan (it may be necessary to grill the aubergines in 2 batches). Grill for 10–15 minutes or until browned and tender, turning once. Meanwhile, mix the flour with a little pepper, and toss the cubes of cheese in the flour until coated on all sides.

5 Remove the aubergine slices from the grill and keep warm. Spread the polenta croutons on one side of the grill pan rack and cook under a moderate heat for 5 minutes, turning them once. Add the cubes of cheese to the other side of the grill rack and cook for a further 5–6 minutes or until the cheese is golden and just beginning to melt at the edges, turning them as they colour.

6 Pour any remaining flavoured oil mixture into a large salad bowl. Add the lettuce, tomatoes, olives, aubergine slices and cheese, and toss together. Scatter with one-third of the polenta croutons and a sprinkling of lemon zest. Serve immediately, with the remaining croutons in a separate bowl.

Each serving provides ⓥ

kcal 404, **protein** 18 g, **fat** 18 g (of which saturated fat 2 g), **carbohydrate** 41 g (of which sugars 7 g), **fibre** 7 g

✓✓✓	B₁, B₆, C, E, folate, niacin, calcium
✓✓	A, zinc
✓	iron, potassium

warm salads

Another idea

• Instead of aubergines, use courgettes, cut diagonally into 1 cm (½ in) slices – they will take about 12 minutes to grill. Infuse the olive oil with a seeded and coarsely chopped fresh red chilli instead of the lemon and herb sprigs. If you like, add another seeded and finely chopped fresh red chilli to the polenta in place of the parsley.

Plus points

• The tomato, which is indigenous to the Andes, was first cultivated in Mexico and brought to Europe in 1523. Today it is one of our most popular fruiting vegetables. It is a good source of the antioxidants vitamin C and beta-carotene, and of several important phytochemicals.
• Made from finely ground corn (maize) meal, polenta is a useful alternative to wheat for anyone on a wheat or gluten-free diet. Polenta is rich in starchy carbohydrate and low in fat.

Hot potato salad with bacon

This piquant salad is a perfect partner for lamb or chicken, or it can be served as an unusual and very tasty starter before a light main course. Scrub the potatoes rather than peel them as many of their vitamins are found just under the skin, and the skin is a valuable source of dietary fibre.

Serves 4

750 g (1 lb 10 oz) small new potatoes, scrubbed

1 can artichoke hearts in brine or water, about 400 g, drained and rinsed

2 tbsp extra virgin olive oil

55 g (2 oz) lean smoked back bacon rashers, derinded and cut into small pieces

1 red onion, cut in half and thinly sliced

1 red or yellow pepper, seeded and cut into thin strips

75 g (2½ oz) rocket

1 tbsp balsamic vinegar

1 tbsp dry white wine

2 tbsp pine nuts, toasted

salt and pepper

Preparation and cooking time: about 35 minutes

Each serving provides

kcal 261, **protein** 10 g, **fat** 9 g (of which saturated fat 2 g), **carbohydrate** 39 g (of which sugars 8 g), **fibre** 3 g

✓✓✓	A, B₁, B₆, C, E, folate, niacin
✓✓	potassium
✓	zinc

1 Cook the potatoes in a saucepan of boiling water for about 15 minutes, depending on size, until just tender. Drain, then cut in half or into quarters if they are large.

2 While the potatoes are cooking, cut the artichoke hearts in half lengthways and pat dry with kitchen paper. Heat half the oil in a non-stick frying pan over a moderately high heat. Place the artichoke hearts in the pan, in a single layer, cut side down, and cook for 2–3 minutes or until golden brown. Turn them over and cook for a further 1 minute or so to brown the other side. Transfer the artichokes to a serving bowl. Add the potatoes and keep warm.

3 Heat the remaining 1 tbsp oil in the frying pan, add the bacon and onion, and cook over a moderately high heat for 1½ minutes, stirring frequently. Add the pepper and continue frying for 1 minute. Using a draining spoon, transfer the bacon, onion and pepper to the serving bowl with the potatoes and artichokes. Put the rocket on top.

4 Return the pan to the heat and add the balsamic vinegar and wine. Tilt the pan to swirl and mix the vinegar and wine with the cooking juices. Pour over the salad, season to taste and turn gently until well combined. Sprinkle with the toasted pine nuts and serve.

Another idea

● For an Italian-style potato and vegetable salad, mix together 2 tbsp finely chopped red onion, 1 finely chopped garlic clove, 4 tbsp extra virgin olive oil and 1 tbsp lemon juice. Add 1 can artichoke hearts, about 400 g, drained, rinsed and halved. Stir to coat with the dressing, then leave to marinate for at least 1 hour. Combine the artichoke hearts and their marinade with the warm potatoes, 2 small raw courgettes, halved and thinly sliced, 12 halved cherry tomatoes, 250 g (8½ oz) cooked green beans, cut into 5 cm (2 in) pieces, and a handful of fresh basil leaves. Mix gently and top with 30 g (1 oz) shavings of Parmesan cheese.

Plus points

● A member of the daisy family, the globe artichoke is an edible thistle native to the Mediterranean region. It was considered a delicacy as far back as Roman times. Artichokes are a useful source of folate and potassium, and they provide calcium and vitamins A and C.

● As well as being an excellent source of vitamin C, red and yellow peppers are rich in phytochemicals that are believed to help protect against the eye disease AMD (age-related macular degeneration).

Griddled asparagus and peppers

Here, spears of asparagus, spring onions and peppers are cooked on a ridged cast-iron grill pan, then mixed with oven-baked Parmesan croutons. If you haven't got a ridged grill pan, the vegetables can be sizzled under the grill instead. Serve as a starter, or as a side salad with grilled chicken or griddled tuna.

Serves 4

500 g (1 lb 2 oz) asparagus spears, woody
   ends trimmed

2 large red peppers, halved and seeded

225 g (8 oz) spring onions

2 tbsp extra virgin olive oil

shavings of Parmesan cheese, about 15 g
   (½ oz) in total, to garnish

Parmesan croutons

2 thick slices of bread, crusts removed and
   diced

1 tbsp extra virgin olive oil

30 g (1 oz) Parmesan cheese, freshly grated

salt and pepper

Lemon and basil dressing

2 tbsp lemon juice

2 tbsp extra virgin olive oil

16 fresh basil leaves, torn into pieces

1 garlic clove, very finely chopped

Preparation and cooking time: 40 minutes

Each serving provides (V)

kcal 296, protein 12 g, fat 19 g (of which saturated fat 5 g), carbohydrate 20 g (of which sugars 11 g), fibre 5 g

✓✓✓	A, B₁, B₆, C, E, folate
✓✓	niacin, calcium, zinc
✓	B₂, iron, potassium

1 Preheat the oven to 180°C (350°F, gas mark 4). Heat a ridged cast-iron grill pan. Put the asparagus, peppers and spring onions in a bowl, add the oil and toss to coat.

2 Arrange the asparagus and peppers in the hot grill pan, in one layer, and cook for 10 minutes or until tender, adding the spring onions after the asparagus and peppers have been cooking for a few minutes. Turn the vegetables frequently so they cook and colour evenly. (You may have to griddle the vegetables in 2 batches, depending on the size of the pan.)

3 Meanwhile, make the croutons. Put the bread in a bowl with the oil and seasoning to taste and toss well. Spread out on a baking tray and bake for about 5 minutes. Sprinkle over the Parmesan cheese and bake for a further 5 minutes or until golden and crisp.

4 Whisk together the dressing ingredients in a salad bowl, adding salt and pepper to taste. Roughly slice the griddled vegetables, add to the bowl and stir to coat with the dressing. Scatter the croutons over the top and garnish with a few shavings of Parmesan. Serve while still warm.

Some more ideas

• For an impressive dinner party starter, leave the griddled asparagus and spring onions whole (omit the peppers) and toss with the dressing. Serve on toasted ciabatta slices with Parmesan shavings scattered over the top.

• To make a griddled mango salad with chilli dressing, peel, stone and slice 1 large mango. Cook on a hot ridged grill pan with 1 red onion and 1 large green pepper, both cut into wedges, for 8–10 minutes or until tender. Chop roughly and put into a bowl with ½ tsp seeded and very finely chopped fresh red chilli, 1 tbsp extra virgin olive oil, 1 tbsp lemon juice and 1 tbsp chopped fresh coriander. Add 45 g (1½ oz) rocket and 25 g (scant 1 oz) cashew nuts, toss well and serve warm.

Plus points

• Parmesan cheese is a good source of protein and a rich source of calcium, needed for strong bones and teeth. Although it has a high fat content, Parmesan also has a very strong and distinctive flavour, so a little goes a long way in a recipe.

• Bread is an important part of a healthy diet as it is a very good source of starchy (complex) carbohydrate. It also contributes vitamins and minerals, particularly calcium, and dietary fibre.

warm salads

Substantial Salads

Satisfying main meals for all the family

It's easy to combine the foods essential for a healthy diet
– carbohydrate-rich rice, potatoes, pasta or couscous, lots
of vegetables and fruit, and modest amounts of protein-
rich foods such as meat, poultry, fish and eggs – in well-
balanced salads that make a meal in themselves.
Combine chicken with sweet potatoes and a spicy
pineapple salsa, or turkey with Indian-spiced rice, grapes
and pecan nuts. Use up roast pork in a salad with new
potatoes, pears and watercress, or roast beef in a rice
salad with sun-dried tomatoes and
mushrooms. Make an Oriental
vegetable and noodle salad topped
with omelette strips, or set soused
fresh sardines on spicy couscous.

Chicken satay salad

Here's a flavourful salad based on the popular Thai dish of satay skewers. Marinated strips of chicken are threaded onto skewers and grilled, then served atop a rice and crunchy vegetable mixture drizzled with a spicy peanut dressing. The chicken can be served on or off the skewers, as you prefer.

Serves 4

550 g (1¼ lb) skinless boneless chicken
   breasts (fillets)

2 tbsp sunflower oil

3 tbsp soy sauce

1 tbsp fish sauce

2 garlic cloves, crushed

2.5 cm (1 in) piece fresh root ginger, finely
   chopped

250 g (8½ oz) basmati rice, well rinsed

100 g (3½ oz) mange-tout, halved

grated zest and juice of 2 limes

2 tbsp chopped fresh coriander

½ small head of Chinese leaves, about 225 g
   (8 oz), shredded

¼ cucumber, diced

4 spring onions, cut into thin strips

Spicy peanut dressing

1 small onion, finely chopped

3 tbsp crunchy peanut butter

1 fresh mild red chilli, seeded and finely
   chopped

100 ml (3½ fl oz) reduced-fat coconut milk

1 tsp caster sugar

Preparation time: about 50 minutes, plus
   at least 3 hours marinating

1 Cut the chicken breasts into long strips about 1 cm (½ in) wide. Mix together half of the oil, 2 tbsp of the soy sauce, the fish sauce, garlic and ginger in a bowl. Add the strips of chicken and toss to coat. Cover and leave to marinate for at least 3 hours.

2 Cook the rice in a saucepan of boiling water for 8 minutes or until almost tender. Add the mange-tout and cook for a further 2 minutes. Drain in a sieve and rinse with cold water.

3 Combine the lime zest and juice with the remaining 1 tbsp oil and soy sauce in a large salad bowl. Add the rice and mange-tout, the chopped coriander, Chinese leaves, cucumber and spring onions, and toss together.

4 Preheat the grill. Lift the strips of chicken out of the marinade, reserving the marinade, and thread onto metal skewers (or onto soaked wooden satay sticks if you want to leave the chicken on them for serving). Grill for 8–10 minutes or until cooked through, turning to brown the chicken evenly.

5 Meanwhile, make the dressing. Put the onion, peanut butter, chilli, coconut milk, sugar and reserved marinade into a small saucepan. Bring to the boil, then cook gently for about 5 minutes, stirring. If the dressing is too thick, add 2–3 tbsp water.

6 Take the chicken off the skewers and add it to the salad (or lay the skewers on top of the salad). Drizzle the dressing over the salad. Serve warm or at cool room temperature.

Plus points

• This salad has everything required for a complete balanced meal, with good amounts of starchy carbohydrates, protein, vitamins and minerals.

• Although peanuts contain large amounts of fat, the majority of it is in the healthy monounsaturated form, which is thought to assist in lowering blood cholesterol levels.

Each serving provides

kcal 574, **protein** 47 g, **fat** 17 g (of which saturated fat 2 g), **carbohydrate** 65 g (of which sugars 6 g), **fibre** 2 g

✓✓✓	B_1, B_6, C, E, niacin
✓✓	B_2, folate, selenium, zinc
✓	iron

substantial salads

Some more ideas

• For a more delicately flavoured dressing, and one that is lower in fat, use the clear liquid, or 'milk', from a coconut instead of coconut milk from a carton. Puncture 2 of the 'eyes' at the top of a coconut using a strong, sharp metal skewer or a screwdriver and a hammer, then drain out the liquid through a sieve.

• For a Thai-style fish and noodle salad, cut 500 g (1 lb 2 oz) monkfish fillet or thick skinless cod fillet into cubes, and marinate and grill as in the main recipe – cooking time will be 5–6 minutes. Instead of basmati rice, cook 250 g (8½ oz) medium Chinese egg noodles in a saucepan of boiling water for 4 minutes, or according to the packet directions, adding the

mange-tout for the last 2 minutes of cooking. In step 3, add 1 red pepper, seeded and cut into strips, with the other vegetables.

• Grill the chicken, then slide it off the skewers and toss with the peanut dressing. Leave to cool, then chill for 2–3 hours. When ready to serve, pile the chicken and dressing on top of the chilled rice salad.

Pork and pear salad with pecans

This is a simple yet substantial salad of new potatoes, crunchy red and white radishes, peppery watercress and juicy pears, topped with slices of roast pork and finished with a scattering of toasted pecan nuts. The dressing is delicately flavoured with ginger juice, squeezed from fresh root ginger.

Serves 4

55 g (2 oz) pecan nuts

900 g (2 lb) even-sized new potatoes, scrubbed

1 small mooli (Japanese white radish), about 170 g (6 oz), peeled and thinly sliced

115 g (4 oz) red radishes, cut into quarters

2 ripe but firm dessert pears

1 Oak Leaf lettuce, separated into leaves

100 g (3½ oz) watercress, tough stalks discarded

340 g (12 oz) roast pork loin, fat removed and thinly sliced

Mustard and ginger dressing

30 g (1 oz) fresh root ginger, peeled and finely chopped

2 tsp wholegrain mustard

2 tsp white wine vinegar

3 tbsp groundnut oil

1 tbsp hazelnut oil

salt and pepper

Preparation time: 35 minutes

Each serving provides

kcal 564, **protein** 37 g, **fat** 26 g (of which saturated fat 5 g), **carbohydrate** 48 g (of which sugars 14 g), **fibre** 6 g

✓✓✓	B_1, B_6, B_{12}, C, E, folate, niacin, zinc
✓✓	B_2, copper, potassium, selenium
✓	A, calcium, iron

1 Heat a frying pan and toast the pecan nuts over a moderate heat for 6–7 minutes. Cool, then chop roughly. Set aside.

2 Cook the potatoes in a saucepan of boiling water for 15 minutes or until tender. Drain. When cool enough to handle, cut into quarters and place in a mixing bowl.

3 To make the dressing, first put the ginger in a garlic crusher and press to squeeze out the juice (this will have to be done in 3 or 4 batches). You need 2 tsp of this ginger juice. Put the ginger juice, mustard, vinegar, groundnut and hazelnut oils, and salt and pepper to taste, in a screwtop jar. Shake well to mix. Pour about one-third of the dressing over the warm potatoes and toss gently to coat. Leave to cool.

4 Meanwhile, in another bowl, toss the mooli and red radishes with half of the remaining dressing, to prevent them from browning. Halve the pears lengthways and scoop out the cores, then cut into long wedges. Toss with the mooli and radishes.

5 Arrange the lettuce leaves and watercress in a shallow salad bowl. Add the mooli mixture to the potatoes and gently mix together. Pile onto the middle of the salad leaves, and arrange the pork slices on top.

6 Stir the toasted pecans into the remaining dressing and drizzle over the top of the salad. Serve immediately.

Some more ideas

• Instead of pears, use other fresh fruit such as 2 peaches or 4 apricots, or 30 g (1 oz) chopped ready-to-eat dried apricots soaked in a little orange or apple juice to plump them up.

• For a pork and apple salad with hazelnuts, replace the pears with red-skinned dessert apples. Instead of mooli and red radishes, cut 150 g (5½ oz) each celeriac and carrots into 5 cm (2 in) long matchstick strips. Finish with toasted hazelnuts instead of pecans.

Plus points

• Pork provides many B vitamins – excellent amounts of B_{12} and good amounts of B_1 and B_6 – and it is a good source of zinc.

• Radishes offer useful amounts of fibre and vitamin C and, in common with other members of the cruciferous family, they contain phytochemicals that may help to protect against cancer. Most of the enzymes responsible for the hot taste are found in the skin – if you find the taste overpowering, peeling will help to reduce the heat.

substantial salads

Roast beef and rice salad

This family-style salad is packed with vitamins, minerals and fibre. It is an excellent way of using up leftover roast beef, and the vegetables can be varied to suit all tastes. It makes a hearty meal in itself.

Serves 4

450 g (1 lb) roast beef, preferably cooked medium-rare or medium, trimmed of fat and cut into 1 cm (½ in) cubes

55 g (2 oz) sun-dried tomatoes in oil, drained and thinly sliced

4 spring onions, thinly sliced

2 tbsp snipped fresh chives

250 g (8½ oz) basmati rice, well rinsed

1 celery stick, thinly sliced

1 carrot, coarsely grated

1 courgette, coarsely grated

75 g (2½ oz) button mushrooms, thinly sliced

4 tbsp chopped fresh flat-leaf parsley

radicchio or other salad leaves to serve (optional)

Cider vinegar dressing

1½ tsp mustard powder

½ tsp caster sugar

2 tbsp cider vinegar

3 tbsp extra virgin olive oil

salt and pepper

Preparation time: about 30 minutes, plus at least 30 minutes marinating and chilling

Each serving provides

kcal 597, **protein** 43 g, **fat** 22 g (of which saturated fat 5 g), **carbohydrate** 55 g (of which sugars 5 g), **fibre** 2 g

✓✓✓	A, B$_1$, B$_6$, B$_{12}$, E, niacin, zinc
✓✓	B$_2$, C, folate, iron
✓	potassium, selenium

1 First make the dressing. Put the mustard powder and sugar in a large mixing bowl and stir in the vinegar until smooth. Whisk in the oil until thoroughly blended. Season with salt and pepper to taste.

2 Add the beef, sun-dried tomatoes, spring onions and chives to the bowl and stir to coat all the ingredients with the dressing. Cover and chill for at least 30 minutes (or up to 8 hours).

3 Meanwhile, cook the rice in a saucepan of boiling water for 8–10 minutes or until just tender. Drain well and spread out on a tray to cool completely.

4 When the rice is cool, transfer it to a bowl and stir in the celery, carrot, courgette, mushrooms and parsley. Cover and chill until required.

5 About 10 minutes before serving, remove the marinated beef and the rice salad from the refrigerator. If you like, line 4 plates with radicchio or other salad leaves. Add the marinated beef mixture to the rice salad and gently stir together until well mixed. Spoon onto the bed of leaves and serve.

Some more ideas

● Make a ham, peach and rice salad, using cubes of cooked ham instead of beef, and replacing the sun-dried tomatoes and onions with 2 sliced peaches and the chives with chopped parsley. In the rice salad, instead of the celery, carrot, courgette and mushrooms, use 200 g (7 oz) thawed frozen sweetcorn kernels, 2 thinly sliced leeks and 200 g (7 oz) chopped fennel.

● Small cubes of a tasty cheese, about 250 g (8½ oz) in total, make a good vegetarian alternative to the beef. Also add some mustard and cress or alfalfa sprouts to the salad.

Plus points

● As a result of modern breeding techniques, beef is now much leaner than it used to be – lean cuts of beef, such as topside, can contain less than 3% fat.

● Rice is an ideal food to include in a healthy diet as it is a low-fat starchy carbohydrate. Starchy foods break down slowly to offer a long-term energy source.

● Extra virgin olive oil is made from the first pressing of top grade olives from which the stones have been removed. It is green in colour, has a rich flavour and is high in monounsaturated fatty acids. These are the kinds of fat that are thought to help lower cholesterol levels in the blood.

substantial salads

Soused fresh sardine salad

Cooking fish – traditionally by frying – and then submerging it in a 'souse' is a very tasty way to prepare it, and was once a means of preserving. Here sardines are grilled and marinated, then served on a Moroccan-spiced couscous, chickpea and pepper salad. It is a perfect prepare-ahead dish for summer entertaining.

Serves 4

8 fresh sardines, cleaned, scaled and heads removed

1 small lemon, cut into 8 thin slices and each slice halved

250 g (8½ oz) couscous

1½ tsp ground coriander

1 tsp turmeric

pinch of cayenne pepper

1½ tsp butter

600 ml (1 pint) boiling water

1 can chickpeas, about 410 g, drained and rinsed

4 spring onions, finely chopped

2 large peppers (1 red and 1 yellow), seeded and finely diced

1 large courgette, grated

140 g (5 oz) baby spinach leaves

fresh flat-leaf parsley to garnish

salt and pepper

Marinade

finely grated zest of 1 large lemon

4 tbsp lemon juice

1 tbsp garlic-flavoured olive oil

1 fresh red or green chilli, seeded and finely chopped

1 shallot, finely chopped

6 black peppercorns, lightly cracked

1 bay leaf

Preparation time: 25 minutes, plus at least 30 minutes marinating

1 Preheat the grill to high. To make the marinade, put the lemon zest and juice in a bowl and whisk in the oil. Stir in the chilli, shallot, peppercorns and bay leaf.

2 Line the grill rack with foil and lightly brush with marinade. Tuck 2 lemon slice halves in each sardine cavity, then arrange the sardines on the foil. Brush with more marinade and grill for 2 minutes.

3 Carefully turn the sardines over, lightly brush with marinade again and grill for a further 2–3 minutes or until the skins are slightly crisp and the flesh flakes easily. Immediately transfer the sardines to a baking dish, arranging them in one layer, and pour over the marinade, including any remaining in the grill pan. Roll each sardine over so it is well coated. Leave to cool, then cover and chill for at least 30 minutes.

4 Meanwhile, put the couscous in a bowl and stir in the coriander, turmeric, cayenne pepper, butter and salt to taste. Pour over the boiling water and stir, then set aside to cool.

5 About 15 minutes before serving, remove the sardines from the fridge. Add the chickpeas, spring onions, peppers and courgette to the couscous, then stir to mix and fluff up the grains.

6 Divide the spinach leaves among 4 plates and spoon on the couscous. Remove the sardines from the marinade and place 2 fish on each plate. Sprinkle with the parsley and serve immediately.

Plus points

• Fresh sardines are an excellent source of vitamin B_{12} and the antioxidant selenium, and also provide useful quantities of potassium.

• The vitamin C in the spinach leaves and the peppers helps with the absorption of iron from the sardines.

• As soon as vegetables are cut, their vitamin content starts to diminish, so if possible they should be prepared just before serving, as is done for this salad.

Each serving provides

kcal 586, **protein** 40 g, **fat** 18 g (of which saturated fat 5 g), **carbohydrate** 68 g (of which sugars 8 g), **fibre** 7 g

---

✓✓✓ A, B_1, B_2, B_6, B_{12}, C, E, folate, niacin, iron, selenium

---

✓✓ calcium, copper, potassium, zinc

Another idea

• Make a soused trout salad with orzo, the small rice-shaped pasta. For the marinade, mix together the finely grated zest of 1 large lemon, 4 tbsp lemon juice, 1 tbsp orange juice, 100 g (3½ oz) thinly sliced shallots, 1 thinly sliced carrot, 1 bay leaf and 1 seeded and chopped fresh green chilli. Grill 4 skinless trout fillets, about 140 g (5 oz) each, for 6–7 minutes, turning once and brushing with the marinade. Transfer the fillets to a baking dish, pour over the marinade and leave to cool, then cover and chill. Meanwhile, cook 250 g (8½ oz) orzo in boiling water for 10–12 minutes, or according to the packet instructions, until al dente. Drain and leave to cool. About 15 minutes before serving, add 85 g (3 oz) baby spinach leaves, 55 g (2 oz) rocket and 1 red pepper, seeded and diced, to the orzo and fold together. Flake the trout and gently stir in, with the marinade, 4 tbsp chopped parsley and seasoning.

Chicken and sweet potatoes

This salad is a riot of tastes, perfect when you are craving wholesome yet interesting food. Slices of chicken and sweet potatoes are served on a bed of leafy greens and vegetables, with a chunky pineapple salsa to spoon over.

Serves 4

900 g (2 lb) sweet potatoes, scrubbed and
    cut into 1 cm (½ in) slices

4 skinless boneless chicken breasts (fillets),
    about 140 g (5 oz) each

pinch each of ground cinnamon and cumin

200 g (7 oz) mixed salad leaves

¼ cucumber, thinly sliced

4 tomatoes, cut into thin wedges

2 tbsp chopped fresh coriander

2 tbsp toasted sunflower seeds

2 spring onions, finely shredded

Pineapple salsa

½ ripe pineapple, about 340 g (12 oz),
    peeled and chopped

½ small red onion, chopped

½ red pepper, seeded and finely diced

2 tbsp chopped fresh mint

¼ tsp mild chilli powder, or to taste

pinch each of ground cinnamon and cumin

juice of ½ lime

Lime and soy dressing

1 tsp caster sugar

juice of ½ lime

2 tbsp sunflower oil

dash of soy sauce, or to taste

Preparation time: 40–45 minutes, plus cooling

1 Cook the sweet potato slices in a saucepan of boiling water for 6–8 minutes or until just tender. Drain and leave to cool.

2 Poach the chicken breasts in simmering water (use the water from the sweet potatoes, if liked) for 4–6 minutes or until cooked through. Drain and leave to cool, then cut into 1 cm (½ in) slices.

3 Put the chicken and sweet potato slices in a bowl and sprinkle with the cinnamon and cumin.

4 To make the salsa, combine the pineapple, red onion, red pepper, mint, chilli powder, cinnamon, cumin and lime juice in a mixing bowl.

5 Whisk together the dressing ingredients in a large shallow salad bowl. Add the salad leaves and toss to coat with the dressing. Arrange the chicken and sweet potato slices, the cucumber slices and tomato wedges on top of the leaves, and scatter over the chopped coriander, sunflower seeds and spring onions. Serve with the pineapple salsa, to be added to taste.

Another idea

• For a smoked chicken and papaya salad, use 350 g (12½ oz) sliced smoked chicken. Make the dressing with 1 tbsp extra virgin olive oil, the juice of 1 lime, a dash of wine vinegar and 1 chopped garlic clove. Arrange the chicken, sweet potatoes and tomato wedges on the dressed salad leaves, together with 1 papaya and 1 avocado, both peeled and sliced, and ½ bulb of fennel, cut into matchstick strips (omit the cucumber and the pineapple salsa). Scatter over the coriander, sunflower seeds and spring onions, and serve.

Plus point

• The sweet potato is native to central America – Columbus was believed to have brought it to Europe after his first voyage to the New World. Sweet potatoes contain slightly more calories than white potatoes, but they provide more vitamin E. They also supply good amounts of vitamin C and potassium as well as dietary fibre. The orange-fleshed variety is an excellent source of beta-carotene.

Each serving provides

kcal 459, protein 25 g, fat 13 g (of which saturated fat 2 g), carbohydrate 65 g (of which sugars 28 g), fibre 9 g

✓✓✓	A, B₁, B₆, C, E, niacin, copper, potassium
✓✓	B₂, folate, iron, selenium, zinc
✓	calcium

substantial salads

Tiger prawns with dill dressing

In this good-looking salad, quickly seared tiger prawns are served piled on a mixture of aromatic basmati and wild rice, crunchy broccoli florets, mange-tout and yellow pepper tossed in a fresh dill and lime juice dressing. Together the ingredients make a well-balanced dish, as healthy as it is delicious.

Serves 4

250 g (8½ oz) mixed basmati and wild rice, well rinsed

thinly pared zest and juice of 1 lime

3 tbsp sunflower oil

2 tsp toasted sesame oil

1 tbsp light soy sauce

125 g (4½ oz) broccoli, broken into small florets

125 g (4½ oz) mange-tout, halved lengthways

400 g (14 oz) raw tiger prawns, peeled but tails left on

1 small yellow pepper, seeded and thinly sliced

75 g (2½ oz) spring onions, sliced

4 tbsp coarsely chopped fresh dill

salt and pepper

Preparation time: 40 minutes, plus cooling

Each serving provides

kcal 393, **protein** 20 g, **fat** 11 g (of which saturated fat 1 g), **carbohydrate** 53 g (of which sugars 2 g), **fibre** 2 g

✓✓✓ B$_1$, B$_6$, B$_{12}$, E, niacin

✓ iron, selenium, zinc

1 Cook the rice with the lime zest in a saucepan of boiling water for 20 minutes, or according to the packet instructions, until tender. Drain the rice and tip it into a wide salad bowl. Discard the lime zest.

2 Whisk together 1 tbsp of the lime juice, 2 tbsp of the sunflower oil, the sesame oil, soy sauce, and salt and pepper to taste in a small bowl. Drizzle this dressing over the rice and stir to mix. Spread out the rice in the bowl and leave to cool.

3 Meanwhile, put the broccoli in a steamer basket set over a pan of boiling water and steam for 4 minutes. Add the mange-tout and steam for a further 2 minutes or until the vegetables are tender but still crisp. Tip the vegetables into a colander and refresh under cold running water.

4 Heat the remaining 1 tbsp of sunflower oil in a large frying pan. Add the prawns and cook over a high heat for 1–2 minutes on each side or until pink and cooked through. Remove from the heat and sprinkle with the remaining lime juice.

5 Add the broccoli, mange-tout, pepper, spring onions and 3 tbsp of the dill to the rice and stir gently to mix. Pile the prawns on top and scatter over the rest of the dill. Serve immediately.

Some more ideas

• The salad can be made in advance and chilled until required. Let it stand at room temperature for 30 minutes before serving.

• For a high-fibre salad, use brown long-grain rice instead of basmati and wild rice.

• Instead of broccoli and mange-tout, use asparagus tips and sliced small courgettes.

• To save time, buy 200 g (7 oz) cooked peeled tiger prawns and simply toss them in the lime juice.

• Instead of prawns, use 16 scallops, searing them in the hot oil for about 1 minute on each side or until golden brown.

• For a Thai dressing, whisk together 5 tbsp reduced-fat coconut milk, 1 tsp toasted sesame oil, 1 tbsp fish sauce, 1 seeded and very finely chopped fresh red chilli and 3 tbsp chopped fresh coriander.

Plus point

• Prawns are low in fat and calories. They contain useful amounts of many of the B vitamins, particularly vitamin B$_{12}$, which is essential for the formation of red blood cells and maintaining a healthy nervous system. They also provide good amounts of copper, phosporus, iodine and the antioxidant selenium, plus small amounts of iron.

substantial salads

94

Salade niçoise

Waxy new potatoes, such as Pink Fir Apple, La Ratte or Charlotte, are ideal for salads such as this classic, as they are firm enough to keep their shape when stirred with other ingredients. Serve with crusty French bread.

Serves 4

500 g (1 lb 2 oz) waxy new potatoes, scrubbed

340 g (12 oz) thin green beans, halved

1 red or yellow pepper, seeded and thinly sliced

1 small bulb of fennel, thinly sliced

4 tuna steaks, 5 cm (2 in) thick, about 400 g (14 oz) in total

1 tsp extra virgin olive oil

lettuce leaves

16 baby plum tomatoes, halved

3 hard-boiled eggs, quartered

12 black olives, stoned

handful of fresh basil leaves, torn if large

salt and pepper

Anchovy dressing

1 can anchovy fillets, about 50 g, drained

1 small garlic clove

2 tsp Dijon mustard

1 tbsp lemon juice

4 tbsp extra virgin olive oil

Preparation time: 45 minutes

Each serving provides

kcal 483, **protein** 37 g, **fat** 25 g (of which saturated fat 5 g), **carbohydrate** 28 g (of which sugars 9 g), **fibre** 5 g

✓✓✓	A, B$_1$, B$_6$, B$_{12}$, C, E, folate, niacin, selenium
✓✓	B$_2$, copper, iron, potassium, zinc
✓	calcium

1 Cook the potatoes in a saucepan of boiling water for 10–15 minutes or until tender, adding the beans for the last 5 minutes of cooking. Drain and refresh under cold running water. Cut the potatoes in half, then transfer the potatoes and beans to a mixing bowl. Add the pepper and fennel.

2 To make the anchovy dressing, put 3 of the anchovy fillets and the peeled garlic in a food processor and process to a purée. Add the mustard, lemon juice and oil, and process until smooth. Alternatively, use a pestle and mortar, pounding the anchovies and garlic to a paste before whisking in the remaining ingredients. Pour the dressing over the vegetables and toss to coat.

3 Brush the tuna steaks with the oil and season with pepper. Heat a non-stick frying pan or ridged cast-iron grill pan. Add the tuna steaks and cook over a moderately high heat for about 4 minutes on each side or until lightly browned. Do not overcook or the tuna will be dry.

4 Make a layer of lettuce leaves on each of 4 plates and divide the potato mixture among them. Top with the tuna steaks. Arrange the tomatoes and egg quarters around the edge and scatter over the olives and basil leaves. Finish with the rest of the anchovies, arranging 2 on top of each serving.

Some more ideas

• Use 2–3 celery sticks instead of fennel.

• Omit the anchovy garnish, and serve the salad with garlic and anchovy croutons. Spread out 8 slices of French bread on a baking sheet and toast under the grill until lightly browned on both sides. Rub one side with a cut garlic clove, then mash an anchovy fillet on top of each and spread as evenly as possible. Cut the slices in halves or into quarters, using a serrated knife, and arrange on the salad plates.

• Replace the fresh tuna with 2 cans tuna in spring water, about 200 g (7 oz) each, drained and broken into chunks.

Plus points

• Fresh tuna contains beneficial omega-3 fatty acids, which reduce the tendency of blood to clot and thus are helpful in preventing and treating heart disease. Tuna is also an excellent source of vitamins D and B$_{12}$ and a useful source of potassium.

• Fennel provides useful amounts of beta-carotene, folate and potassium, as well as cancer-fighting phytochemicals.

• Green beans are a good source of folate and dietary fibre.

Three beans and rice

Three bean salad is an American classic that can be found in delis across the land. It is easy to make and very nutritious. By adding rice and more vegetables, it becomes a substantial main dish, packed with dietary fibre, starchy carbohydrate, vitamins and minerals, and providing a good amount of protein.

Serves 4

250 g (8½ oz) long-grain rice

2 carrots, thinly sliced

125 g (4½ oz) thin green beans, cut into
  2.5 cm (1 in) lengths

1 can red kidney beans, about 400 g, drained
  and rinsed

1 can black-eyed beans, about 400 g, drained
  and rinsed

1 can chickpeas, about 410 g, drained and
  rinsed

1 large ripe tomato, coarsely chopped

1 small red pepper, seeded and chopped

1 small red onion, chopped

1 tbsp sunflower oil

1 tbsp mild wholegrain mustard

2 tsp caster sugar

3 tbsp red wine vinegar, or to taste

1 tbsp chopped fresh thyme

1 garlic clove, chopped

salt and pepper

Preparation time: about 50 minutes

Each serving provides Ⓥ

kcal 503, **protein** 27 g, **fat** 8 g (of which
saturated fat 1 g), **carbohydrate** 85 g (of
which sugars 17 g), **fibre** 18 g

✓✓✓	A, B₁, B₆, C, E, folate, niacin
✓✓	calcium, iron, potassium, zinc
✓	B₁₂, selenium

1 Put the rice in a saucepan, cover with water and bring to the boil. Reduce the heat and simmer for about 15 minutes, or according to the packet instructions, until tender. Drain and leave to cool.

2 Meanwhile, drop the carrots into another pan of boiling water and cook for 3 minutes. Add the green beans and cook for a further 4 minutes or until the vegetables are tender. Drain and refresh under cold running water.

3 Place the carrots and green beans in a mixing bowl and add the kidney beans, black-eyed beans, chickpeas, tomato, red pepper and red onion.

4 Whisk together the oil, mustard, sugar, vinegar, thyme, garlic, and salt and pepper to taste in a small bowl. Drizzle this dressing over the bean salad and toss well to combine everything. Serve the bean salad over the rice, or gently fold the rice into the bean salad.

Some more ideas

● Replace the green beans with 200 g (7 oz) broccoli, broken into small florets.

● Make a Mexican-style bean and sweetcorn salad. Combine 400 g (14 oz) cooked frozen sweetcorn kernels, drained, with 1 can pinto or borlotti beans, about 400 g, drained and rinsed. Add 1 small red and 1 small green pepper, both seeded and chopped, 1 chopped large ripe tomato, 3 spring onions, sliced, 3 tbsp chopped fresh coriander and 75 g (2½ oz) diced mature Cheddar cheese. Make the dressing with 2 tbsp extra virgin olive oil, the juice of 1 large lime, 2 chopped garlic cloves, ½ tsp mild chilli powder, ½ tsp ground cumin and seasoning to taste. Add to the salad and toss well. Toast 3 corn tortillas under a hot grill for 1 minute or until crisp, then crumble them over the salad.

Plus points

● This salad provides excellent amounts of fibre – both the soluble and insoluble types. Despite the fact that fibre passes through the digestive tract largely undigested, it plays an important role in keeping us fit and healthy by helping to prevent problems such as constipation, diverticulitis, haemorrhoids and colon cancer. Studies have shown that butyrate – a fatty acid formed when fibre is fermented by bacteria in the gut – can cause malignant tumours to self-destruct.

● Carrots were known to the Greeks and Romans, although they were not widely used in Europe until the Middle Ages. Early varieties were red, purple or black – the familiar orange variety was developed in Holland in the 17th century. Carrots are one of the richest sources of beta-carotene and they provide useful amounts of dietary fibre.

Indian-style rice with turkey

The spicy aromas of this satisfying salad make it tempting fare at any time of year. The rice, with its slightly chewy texture and Indian spicing, provides the perfect backdrop for tender turkey (or chicken), crunchy raw vegetables, sweet grapes and toasted nuts. It's a great way to use up leftover roast poultry.

Serves 6

1 tbsp sunflower oil

375 g (13 oz) brown basmati rice, well rinsed

1 onion, finely chopped

1 tsp grated fresh root ginger

¼ tsp garam masala

¼ tsp ground coriander

½ tsp medium-strength curry powder (or mild or hot, if preferred)

750 ml (1¼ pints) hot chicken or vegetable stock, or water

1 bay leaf

3 large celery sticks, chopped

4 spring onions, chopped

1 large carrot, grated

140 g (5 oz) seedless red grapes, halved

500 g (1 lb 2 oz) skinless cooked turkey or chicken meat, cubed

3 tbsp chopped parsley

Oak Leaf or other soft lettuce leaves

75 g (2½ oz) toasted pecan nuts, roughly chopped, or toasted flaked almonds

Citrus vinaigrette

4 tbsp orange juice

2 tsp lime juice

4 tsp sunflower oil

1 tbsp snipped fresh chives

salt and pepper

Preparation time: 50 minutes, plus cooling

1 Heat the oil in a large saucepan over a moderate heat. Add the rice and stir to coat thoroughly, then cook, stirring frequently, for 1 minute. Add the onion, ginger, garam masala, coriander and curry powder, and continue cooking for 3–4 minutes, stirring, until the onion starts to soften.

2 Add the stock or water and bay leaf, and bring to the boil. Reduce the heat, cover and simmer for about 25 minutes or until the rice is tender. Discard the bay leaf and transfer the rice to a large bowl to cool.

3 Meanwhile, to make the dressing, whisk together the orange and lime juices, oil and chives. Season with salt and pepper to taste.

4 Add the celery, spring onions and carrot to the cooled rice. Reserve half the grapes and add the remainder to the rice together with the chicken or turkey and the parsley. Drizzle over the dressing and turn the salad gently to combine everything.

5 Arrange a bed of lettuce leaves on each of 4 plates and pile the rice salad on top. Scatter the remaining grapes and the pecan nuts or almonds over the salad and serve.

Plus points

• Unlike white rice, brown rice retains the germ and bran of the rice grain and therefore contains higher levels of the B vitamins and almost 4 times as much fibre as white rice.

• Grapes provide useful amounts of potassium and a variety of phytochemicals that help to protect against heart disease and cancer. Naturopaths consider grapes to have healing and regenerative properties.

• Without the skin, turkey is very low in fat, and it contains more vitamin B_{12}, niacin and zinc than chicken.

Each serving provides

kcal 475, **protein** 27 g, **fat** 16 g (of which saturated fat 2 g), **carbohydrate** 61 g (of which sugars 10 g), fibre 3 g

✓✓✓	A, B_1, B_{12}, E, niacin, copper
✓✓	C, folate
✓	potassium

Some more ideas

• Peel 3 oranges and divide into segments, working over a bowl to catch the juice. Use the juice in the dressing and garnish the salads with the orange segments.

• For a herby brown rice salad with salmon, cook the rice with the onion as in the main recipe, using fish stock if you wish, but omitting the spices and ginger. Leave to cool, then stir in mixed fresh herbs – 1 tbsp chopped fresh tarragon or dill, 2 tbsp snipped fresh chives and 4 tbsp chopped parsley – plus a 12 cm (5 in) piece of cucumber, quartered lengthways and sliced, 1 large grated carrot, 3 sliced celery sticks and 2 heads of chicory, slivered, or 5 radicchio leaves, torn into thin ribbons. Dress with the citrus vinaigrette and toss gently to combine. Heat 1 tsp extra virgin olive oil in a small frying pan and sauté 400 g (14 oz) skinless salmon fillet for 3 minutes on each side or until just cooked through. Break into large flakes and fold very gently into the rice salad, taking care not to break up the fish too much. Garnish with halved cherry tomatoes.

Noodle and omelette salad

Tasty Oriental flavours mingle in this layered salad. Colourful, crisp vegetables are topped with Chinese egg noodles, broccoli and bean sprouts, and strips of savoury flat omelette are the finishing touch.

Serves 4

225 g (8 oz) broccoli, broken into small florets

250 g (8½ oz) medium Chinese egg noodles

250 g (8½ oz) bean sprouts

250 g (8½ oz) young pak choy, shredded

6 eggs

1 tbsp milk or water

1 tsp soy sauce

2 tsp sunflower oil

1 can water chestnuts, about 220 g, drained
   and sliced or quartered

1 carrot, coarsely grated

1 red pepper, seeded and thinly sliced

5 spring onions, thinly sliced

3 tbsp coarsely chopped fresh coriander

3 tbsp sesame seeds

Rice vinegar dressing

2 tsp caster sugar

3 tbsp rice vinegar

1½ tbsp soy sauce

2 tbsp toasted sesame oil

1 tbsp grated fresh root ginger

salt and pepper

Preparation time: 35–40 minutes

1 Drop the broccoli into a large saucepan of boiling water and boil for 10 seconds. Add the noodles to the pan, breaking them up as you drop them into the boiling water, then remove from the heat. Add the beans sprouts and leave to soak for 4 minutes.

2 Add the pak choy to the pan of hot water and stir round to wilt slightly, then drain the noodles and vegetables well. Transfer to a mixing bowl.

3 Lightly beat the eggs with the milk or water and the soy sauce. Heat ½ tsp of the sunflower oil in an 18 cm (7 in) non-stick omelette pan and add one-quarter of the egg mixture. Cook for about 2 minutes, stirring gently and lifting the edges of the omelette to let the uncooked egg mixture run onto the pan, until the omelette is set. Slide onto a plate. Repeat to make another 3 omelettes, removing them and stacking them as they are cooked. When they are all ready, cut them into thin strips.

4 To make the dressing, whisk together the sugar, vinegar, soy sauce, sesame oil, ginger, and salt and pepper to taste in a large mixing bowl. Drizzle half the dressing over the noodle mixture and toss. Add the water chestnuts, carrot and red pepper to the remaining dressing in the bowl and toss well to coat the vegetables.

5 Arrange the carrot salad on a platter and spoon the noodle salad on top. Sprinkle with the spring onions, coriander and sesame seeds, then add the omelette strips. Serve immediately.

Plus points

• Peppers have a naturally waxy skin, which helps to protect them against oxidation and stops vitamin C from being lost during storage, so their vitamin C content remains high, even several weeks after harvesting. Store peppers in the fridge to keep them fresh for longer.

• Eggs are an inexpensive source of protein and they provide useful amounts of vitamins A, B_2, B_{12}, E and niacin. Although they contain cholesterol, recent studies suggest that unless you suffer from diabetes you can safely eat up to 7 eggs a week without increasing the risk of heart disease or stroke.

Each serving provides ⓥ

kcal 590, **protein** 28 g, **fat** 26 g (of which saturated fat 7 g), **carbohydrate** 63 g (of which sugars 15 g), **fibre** 7 g

✓✓✓	A, B_1, B_2, B_6, B_{12}, C, E, folate, niacin, copper, zinc
✓✓	calcium, iron, potassium
✓	selenium

substantial salads

Another idea

• Make a sweet and sour rice noodle salad with tofu. Place 250 g (8½ oz) rice noodles in a heatproof bowl, pour over boiling water and leave to soak for 3 minutes. Add 100 g (3½ oz) bean sprouts and soak for a further minute. Drain well and dress with 1 tsp soy sauce and 2 tsp toasted sesame oil. Instead of making omelettes, hard-boil 4 eggs and cut them into wedges. For the dressing, purée ½ chopped cucumber in a food processor or blender, then add 1–2 chopped garlic cloves, 2 tbsp sunflower oil, 3 tbsp cider or wine vinegar, 4 tsp caster sugar and seasoning to taste, and process again to mix. Taste for sweet and sour balance. Arrange ½ cucumber, sliced, 340 g (12 oz) red cabbage, shredded, 170 g (6 oz) baby spinach leaves and 2 grated carrots on a serving platter or plates. Add the egg wedges, 200 g (7 oz) plain or marinated tofu, cut into bite-sized pieces, and the noodles and bean sprouts. Sprinkle with 1 tbsp chopped unsalted roasted peanuts. Serve with the sweet and sour cucumber dressing.

Special Salads

Starters and main dishes for entertaining

A dazzling selection of fresh fruits and vegetables from all over the world is available now the whole year round, making it easy to create a fantastic variety of special salads. Set the taste buds tingling with a starter salad of beetroot and pepper topped with grilled goat's cheese on toasted French bread, or try a salad of wild mushrooms and poached quail's eggs served with walnut bread. For an exotic salad lunch, try Teriyaki-glazed prawns set atop crunchy vegetables, or capture the flavour of Middle Eastern cooking with a colourful squash couscous. And why not impress your friends with sweet and sour duck served with rice and fruit?

Grilled goat's cheese salad

Crisp toasted French bread is spread with a rich red onion marmalade flavoured with balsamic vinegar and rosemary, then topped with creamy goat's cheese and finished under the grill. Served with a beetroot, pepper and lamb's lettuce salad, this makes an impressive starter.

Serves 4

1 tbsp extra virgin olive oil

4 small red onions, about 300 g (10½ oz) in total, thinly sliced

2 garlic cloves, finely chopped

1 tsp sugar

2 tsp balsamic vinegar

4 slices French bread, about 115 g (4 oz) in total

few sprigs of fresh rosemary

200 g (7 oz) goat's cheese, cut into 4 slices

85 g (3 oz) lamb's lettuce

115 g (4 oz) cooked beetroot, peeled and cut into thin strips

1 small red pepper, seeded and cut into thin strips

salt and pepper

Balsamic dressing

2 tbsp extra virgin olive oil

2 tsp balsamic vinegar

Preparation time: 25 minutes

1 Preheat the grill. Heat the oil in a frying pan, add the onions and cook for 5 minutes, stirring occasionally, until softened. Add the garlic and sugar, and cook for a further 5–8 minutes, stirring frequently, until the onions are very soft, browned and caramelised. Stir in the balsamic vinegar.

2 Lightly toast the French bread on both sides under the grill. Divide the onion marmalade among the slices. Top each with a few rosemary leaves and then a slice of goat's cheese. Add a sprinkling of pepper.

3 Cook the cheesy toasts under the hot grill for 3–4 minutes or until the cheese is bubbling.

4 Meanwhile, to make the dressing, whisk the oil, vinegar and salt and pepper to taste in a mixing bowl. Add the lamb's lettuce, beetroot and red pepper and toss. Divide among 4 plates. Top with the goat's cheese toasts, garnish with rosemary and serve.

Some more ideas

• Try baby spinach or baby red chard leaves in place of lamb's lettuce.

• Instead of onion marmalade, rub the slices of toasted French bread with 1 cut garlic clove, then spread with 4 tsp sun-dried tomato paste. Top with the goat's cheese and grill. Serve with a salad made from 1 small Oak Leaf lettuce, torn into bite-sized pieces, 225 g (8 oz) halved cherry tomatoes and 1 red pepper, seeded and cut into thin strips, tossed in a dressing made with 3 tbsp extra virgin olive oil, 1 tbsp red wine vinegar, 2 tsp sun-dried tomato paste and seasoning to taste. Garnish the toasts with fresh basil leaves.

• Top the toast slices with goat's cheese and add a drizzle of walnut or hazelnut oil (omit the onion marmalade and rosemary). Grill, then serve on a bed of mixed green salad leaves tossed with toasted walnuts or hazelnuts and a vinaigrette made with extra virgin olive oil and a little walnut or hazelnut oil.

Plus points

• Beetroot is a good source of folate, which is needed during the early stages of pregnancy to reduce the risk of spina bifida. It is also rich in potassium, a good intake of which can help to balance out the adverse effect of a high salt intake on blood pressure. The leafy tops of beetroot can be cooked and served like spinach.

• Red onions have been shown to contain higher levels of flavonoids – compounds that may help to protect against heart disease – than white onions.

Each serving provides

kcal 307, **protein** 11 g, **fat** 17 g (of which saturated fat 7 g), **carbohydrate** 28 g (of which sugars 10 g), **fibre** 3 g

✓✓✓	A, B$_1$, B$_6$, B$_{12}$, C, E, niacin
✓✓	B$_2$, folate
✓	calcium, selenium

special salads

Mushrooms and quail's eggs

Many 'wild' mushrooms are now cultivated, so they are readily available. Here, full-flavoured shiitake mushrooms are gently poached with more delicate chanterelles and oyster mushrooms, then tossed with salad herbs and topped with softly poached quail's eggs. Try this delicious starter salad with warm walnut bread.

Serves 4

2 shallots, thinly sliced

1 garlic clove, crushed

1 tsp coriander seeds, crushed

1 bay leaf

200 ml (7 fl oz) vegetable stock

115 g (4 oz) shiitake mushrooms

115 g (4 oz) oyster mushrooms

115 g (4 oz) chanterelles

2 tbsp marsala or medium sherry

140 g (5 oz) baby leeks, or 1 medium leek, cut into 2.5 cm (1 in) lengths

1 tbsp truffle or walnut oil

1 tsp lemon juice

12 quail's eggs

1 Oak Leaf lettuce, separated into leaves

85 g (3 oz) mixed fresh salad herbs, such as salad burnet, rocket, sorrel and flat-leaf parsley

pepper

Preparation time: 45 minutes

Each serving provides ⓥ

kcal 200, **protein** 15 g, **fat** 14 g (of which saturated fat 3 g), **carbohydrate** 3 g (of which sugars 3 g), **fibre** 3 g

✓✓✓	B_1, B_2, B_6, C, E, niacin
✓✓	A, folate, copper, iron
✓	calcium, potassium

1 Put the shallots, garlic, crushed coriander seeds and bay leaf in a large saucepan. Add the stock and bring to the boil, then cover and simmer for 10 minutes.

2 Meanwhile, thickly slice the shiitake mushrooms, and break the oyster mushrooms and chanterelles into smaller pieces – leave small ones whole.

3 Add the marsala or sherry and the shiitake mushrooms to the stock. Simmer gently, uncovered, for about 3 minutes. Add the chanterelles and oyster mushrooms, and cook for a further 1–2 minutes or until just tender.

4 Remove the mushrooms using a draining spoon, with any bits of shallot or coriander clinging to them, and transfer to a salad bowl.

5 Add the leeks to the stock and simmer for 3–4 minutes or until tender. Remove with a draining spoon and add to the mushrooms.

6 Rapidly boil the stock for about 5 minutes or until syrupy and reduced to about 5 tbsp. Strain the liquid through a very fine sieve into a jug (this will remove any bits of grit you may have missed when cleaning the mushrooms). Whisk in the oil, lemon juice and pepper to taste. Pour 3 tbsp of this dressing over the mushrooms and leeks and toss gently. Leave to cool.

7 Meanwhile, cook the quail's eggs in boiling water for 1–2 minutes, depending on whether you prefer them soft or medium boiled. Plunge into cold water to cool, then peel.

8 Put the lettuce leaves and herbs in a mixing bowl. Drizzle over the remaining dressing and toss to coat. Arrange the salad leaves on one side of 4 plates and the mushroom mixture on the other side. Cut the quail's eggs in half and place 6 halves on each plate. Serve at once.

Plus point

• There are more than 2500 varieties of mushrooms grown worldwide, and many supermarkets are now stocking some of the more exotic varieties such as cep or porcini, chanterelle, oyster and shiitake. All varieties of mushroom are low in fat and calories, but provide useful amounts of the B vitamins niacin, B_6 and folate. They are also a good source of copper, which aids the absorption of iron and potassium and thus helps to regulate blood pressure.

Another idea

• For a delicious marinated mushroom and fennel salad, cut 140 g (5 oz) portabella or chestnut mushrooms into thick wedges and place in a bowl with 140 g (5 oz) whole baby button mushrooms, a thinly sliced bulb of fennel and 2 bay leaves. Crush a clove of garlic and 4 juniper berries in a mortar with a pestle.

Mix with 2 tbsp extra virgin olive oil, 1 tbsp walnut oil, 2 tsp white wine vinegar, and salt and pepper to taste. Pour over the mushrooms and fennel and toss to coat. Cover and marinate in the fridge for 2 hours. Remove and discard the bay leaves. Put 30 g (1 oz) rocket leaves in a blender with 75 ml (2½ fl oz) extra virgin olive oil and blend together until smooth. Strain the

oil through a fine sieve – it will now be a vibrant green colour. Drizzle 1 tbsp of the rocket oil over the mushrooms, then scatter on croutons (see Some More Ideas, Chicken Caesar salad, page 39). Serve with chunks of warm ciabatta bread. Store the remaining rocket oil in a screw-top jar in the fridge for up to 2 weeks. Use it with chicken, fish or tomato salads.

Figs with Parma ham

Luscious ripe figs go so well with lean Parma ham, and make an elegant little starter salad. In this delectable version, the vitamin content is boosted with the addition of green beans and bulb fennel, plus some fresh pineapple for an unexpected touch of tangy sweetness.

Serves 4

50 g (1¾ oz) thin green beans

100 g (3½ oz) mixed salad leaves, such as frisée and rocket

2 tbsp chopped fresh mint

¼ bulb of fennel, cut into thin strips

2 shallots, finely chopped

6 ripe fresh figs, cut in half

90 g (3¼ oz) Parma ham, fat removed and cut into thin strips

1 large slice of pineapple, about 140 g (5 oz), cut into small strips

Balsamic and lemon dressing

2 tbsp extra virgin olive oil

1 tbsp balsamic vinegar

juice of ½ lemon

salt and pepper

Preparation time: 15 minutes

1 Drop the beans into a saucepan of boiling water and cook for just 2 minutes. Drain and refresh under cold running water.

2 To make the dressing, whisk together the olive oil, vinegar and lemon juice in a mixing bowl, and season with salt and pepper to taste. Add the green beans, salad leaves, mint, fennel and shallots, and toss to coat everything with the dressing. Arrange the bean and fennel salad on 4 plates or a serving platter.

3 Place the fig halves on the plates or platter. Add a mound of shredded Parma ham and a mound of pineapple beside them. Serve immediately.

Another idea

● For a hot grilled fig salad with ricotta, arrange the fig halves, cut side up, in a grill pan and sprinkle with 1–2 tsp sugar. Grill until the figs are warmed through and lightly browned and caramelised. Place the figs on the bean salad and dot them with 75 g (2½ oz) ricotta cheese. Instead of Parma ham and pineapple, cut 1 juicy, ripe dessert pear into matchstick strips, and pile next to the figs, with 30 g (1 oz) fresh Parmesan cheese shavings.

Plus point

● Fresh pineapple contains a substance called bromelain, a digestive enzyme that can break down proteins and can be used to tenderise meat. There is some evidence to suggest that bromelain may help to break up blood clots and therefore may be helpful in protecting against heart disease. Bromelain has an anti-inflammatory action and has been used in the treatment of arthritis. It is also believed to speed up the repair of damaged tissues.

Each serving provides

kcal 154, **protein** 8 g, **fat** 9 g (of which saturated fat 2 g), **carbohydrate** 11 g (of which sugars 11 g), **fibre** 2 g

✓✓✓ B_1, B_6, E, niacin

✓✓   C

special salads

Oriental broccoli salad

In this delicious vegetarian salad, tiny florets of broccoli, baby corn and sugarsnap peas are blanched briefly and then tossed with crunchy raw vegetables in a soy and peanut butter dressing. Nutty-flavoured roasted kasha (buckwheat grain) adds texture. Serve as a starter with rye or pumpernickel bread.

Serves 4

300 g (10½ oz) small broccoli florets

200 g (7 oz) small sugarsnap peas

125 g (4½ oz) baby corn, halved lengthways

1 bunch of spring onions, shredded

1 red pepper, seeded and diced

100 g (3½ oz) young, tender pak choy leaves, halved lengthways if large

85 g (3 oz) bean sprouts

2 tbsp roasted kasha (buckwheat grain)

Peanut butter dressing

4 tbsp crunchy peanut butter

5 tbsp warm water

juice of 1 lemon

2 tbsp light soy sauce

¼ tsp caster sugar

1 tsp finely grated fresh root ginger

Preparation time: about 25 minutes

Each serving provides Ⓥ

kcal 190, **protein** 12 g, **fat** 8 g (of which saturated fat 1 g), **carbohydrate** 20 g (of which sugars 9 g), **fibre** 6 g

✓✓✓	A, B₁, B₆, C, E, folate
✓✓	niacin, copper, zinc
✓	B₂, iron

1 Whisk all the dressing ingredients together in a large salad bowl.

2 Drop the broccoli florets, sugarsnap peas and baby corn into a saucepan of boiling water and blanch for about 2 minutes or until the vegetables are slightly softened, but still crisp. Drain and refresh under cold running water.

3 Add the blanched vegetables to the salad bowl together with the spring onions, red pepper, pak choy and bean sprouts. Toss well to coat with the dressing. Serve immediately, with the kasha to be sprinkled over the top.

Some more ideas

• Replace the bean sprouts with 1 can water chestnuts, about 200 g, drained and chopped.

• For a broccoli and pasta salad to serve 4 as a main dish, make the dressing with tahini instead of peanut butter and flavour with 1 large crushed garlic clove and 8 shredded fresh basil leaves in place of the sugar and ginger. Cook 225 g (8 oz) orecchiette (little pasta ears) in boiling water for 10–12 minutes, adding the broccoli florets for the last 3 minutes of cooking. Drain well. Toss the pasta and broccoli into the dressing with the spring onions and red peppers, 2 tbsp capers, 8 chopped sun-dried tomatoes and 225 g (8 oz) halved cherry tomatoes (omit the sugarsnap peas, baby corn, pak choy and bean sprouts). Instead of kasha, sprinkle on 2 tbsp toasted pine nuts.

Plus points

• Broccoli is an excellent source of the antioxidants beta-carotene and vitamin C, and provides good amounts of the B vitamins B₆, folate and niacin. It also contains a variety of phytochemicals, which studies suggest may help to protect against cancer.

• Peanuts are a good source of protein, niacin and phosphorus. New research suggests that peanuts are also rich in a group of cancer-fighting compounds called phytosterols.

• Sugarsnap peas are a good source of vitamin C, and offer more soluble fibre than ordinary peas as they are eaten pod and all.

Fresh artichoke and crab salad

This salad is a real treat when globe artichokes are in season. The large outer leaves are removed and the succulent, meaty bottom part, or heart, is cooked, then served with fresh crab meat in a lemony dressing.

Serves 4

4 large globe artichokes, about 340 g (12 oz) each

2 lemons, halved

Herb vinaigrette

1 tbsp lemon juice

3 tbsp extra virgin olive oil

1 tbsp finely chopped fresh chervil or parsley

1 tbsp finely chopped fresh chives

salt and pepper

Crab salad

2 tbsp plain low-fat yogurt

2 tbsp mayonnaise

½ tsp grated lemon zest

1 tsp lemon juice

1½ tbsp finely chopped fresh chives

450 g (1 lb) fresh crab meat, preferably white

Little Gem lettuce leaves to serve

Preparation time: 1½ hours, plus cooling

Each serving provides

kcal 323, **protein** 30 g, **fat** 20 g (of which saturated fat 3 g), **carbohydrate** 10 g (of which sugars 5 g), **fibre** 5 g

✓✓✓	B_1, B_2, B_6, E, folate, niacin, copper, zinc
✓✓	iron, potassium, selenium
✓	A, C

1 To prepare each artichoke, cut off the top two-thirds and trim the stalk level with the base. Rub the cut surfaces with lemon juice as you work. Pull off the large outer leaves, starting from the bottom, to expose the soft, pale inner leaves. Holding the artichoke in one hand, trim the top edge to form a rounded shape, and trim around the sides and base to remove all the green parts and expose the pale yellow flesh. Drop the artichoke into a bowl of water with the juice of ½ lemon added to it. Prepare the remaining artichokes in the same way.

2 Put the artichokes in a saucepan large enough to hold them in a single layer, cover with boiling water and add the juice of ½ lemon. Cover the pan and simmer for about 40 minutes or until a leaf can be pulled away easily and the hearts are tender. Remove from the pan and leave to drain upside down until cool.

3 To make the herb vinaigrette, put the lemon juice in a bowl, whisk in the olive oil and season with salt and pepper to taste. Stir in the chervil or parsley and chives.

4 Quarter the artichokes and use a teaspoon to scoop out the fuzzy choke just underneath the centre leaves. Add the artichoke pieces to the herb vinaigrette and turn to coat.

5 For the crab salad, put the yogurt, mayonnaise, lemon zest and juice, and chives in a mixing bowl and stir to combine. Add the crab and mix in gently. Taste and add more lemon juice if you wish.

6 Arrange 2–3 lettuce leaves on each of 4 plates to form a small bed or cup and spoon on the crab salad. Add the artichoke quarters with their dressing, and serve at once.

Plus points

• Crab, like other shellfish, is a good source of low-fat protein. It also provides useful amounts of vitamin B_2, potassium and zinc.

• Chives are a member of the same family as onions and garlic and share the same antibiotic healing powers.

• Globe artichokes are rich in cynarin, a phytochemical that is believed to help reduce high blood cholesterol levels and to help the liver excrete toxins from the body.

special salads

Some more ideas

● Young purple-tinged artichokes, about 6 cm (2½ in) tall, are beautifully tender and almost all parts are edible. When they are in season, use 12 of them, about 675 g (1½ lb) in total, for this salad. To prepare, pull off the bottom 2 or 3 rows of outer leaves, as well as any damaged leaves, trim the stalk close to the base and cut off the top third. Simmer the artichokes for about 30 minutes, then cut in half.

● Make an artichoke, mushroom and smoked ham salad, replacing the crab meat with 200 g (7 oz) thinly sliced button mushrooms and 300 g (10½ oz) smoked ham, cut into thin slivers. Use 1 tsp grated lemon zest in the dressing for the mushroom and ham salad, and also add 1–2 tsp Dijon mustard. Cut the artichokes into eighths, and instead of tossing them in the herb vinaigrette, fold them into the mushroom and ham salad. Pile onto lettuce leaves, and garnish with a good sprinkling of chopped fresh chives and chervil or parsley.

● Use fromage frais in the dressing for the crab salad instead of yogurt.

Teriyaki-glazed prawn salad

East meets West in this intriguing salad of tiger prawns, Parma ham, courgettes, tomatoes and Chinese leaves in a Japanese-style dressing. Serve it as a stylish lunch dish, with French bread or ciabatta.

Serves 4

4 paper-thin slices Parma ham, about 45 g (1½ oz) in total, trimmed of excess fat

12 large raw tiger prawns, about 400 g (14 oz) in total, peeled but tails left on

1 courgette, cut into 16 slices

12 cherry tomatoes

1 tbsp toasted sesame oil

1 tbsp sunflower oil

225 g (8 oz) Chinese leaves, shredded

100 g (3½ oz) baby spinach leaves

4 spring onions, green part only, chopped

4 tbsp snipped fresh chives

4 tbsp chopped fresh flat-leaf parsley

4 tbsp chopped fresh coriander

2 tbsp sesame seeds

1 orange, cut into wedges, to garnish

Teriyaki-style glaze

juice of 1 large orange

2 tbsp sake or dry sherry

1 tbsp soft light brown sugar

1½ tsp soy sauce

1 garlic clove, crushed

Preparation time: 45 minutes

Each serving provides

kcal 245, **protein** 23 g, **fat** 11 g (of which saturated fat 2 g), **carbohydrate** 12 g (of which sugars 11 g), **fibre** 3 g

✓✓✓	B₁, B₆, B₁₂, C, E, folate, niacin
✓✓	calcium, copper, selenium, zinc
✓	iron

1 Place all the ingredients for the glaze in a small bowl and stir to dissolve the sugar. Set aside.

2 Preheat the grill to high, and line the grill pan with foil. Cut each slice of Parma ham lengthways into 3 strips, so you have 12 long strips. Wrap a strip around each prawn, pressing the ham so it stays in position.

3 Thread the prawns, courgette slices and cherry tomatoes onto 4 metal skewers, alternating the ingredients so you start and finish with courgette slices. Pour half the glaze into a large mixing bowl and reserve for making the dressing. Generously brush some of the remaining glaze over the ingredients on the skewers, then place on the grill rack.

4 Brush the skewers again with the glaze and grill for 3 minutes. Turn the skewers over and brush with the remaining glaze. Grill for another 3 minutes or until the prawns are pink.

5 Meanwhile, add the sesame oil and sunflower oil to the reserved glaze and whisk to mix. Add the Chinese leaves, spinach, spring onions, chives, parsley and coriander. Toss everything together to coat with the dressing.

6 Divide the salad among 4 plates. Place a kebab on each plate, and remove the skewers, if liked. Sprinkle with the sesame seeds and serve at once, garnished with orange wedges.

Another idea

● For a Mediterranean balsamic-glazed scallop salad, replace the tiger prawns with 12 large scallops, wrapping them in Parma ham in the same way. Instead of courgettes, use 1 can artichoke hearts, about 400 g, drained. Make the glaze with 2 tbsp extra virgin olive oil, 1 tbsp balsamic vinegar, a splash of orange juice and ½ tsp crushed dried chillies, or to taste. Use 1½–2 tsp to baste the kebabs while they grill, allowing about 3 minutes on each side; use the rest of the glaze to dress 2 thinly sliced red, yellow or orange peppers, 1–2 thinly sliced courgettes and 75 g (2½ oz) rocket. Serve the skewer ingredients on the salad.

Plus points

● Parma ham, the most famous of the Italian salted, air-dried prosciuttos, is a good lean alternative to bacon rashers, as long as you trim off all the fat.

● Spring onions contain vitamin C, which helps your body absorb the iron from the prawns in this salad.

● Sesame seeds come from a herbaceous plant native to Indonesia and East Africa – the first known evidence of its cultivation is from the Middle East in 3000BC. As well as contributing a distinctive flavour, they provide useful amounts of calcium.

special salads

Scallop salad with ginger

This unusual and very nutritious salad is based on soba, the Japanese noodles made from buckwheat. They are tossed with bean sprouts, Chinese leaves, fresh coriander and an intensely flavoured dressing, then topped with juicy soy-grilled scallops and mushrooms and a garnish of fine shreds of nori seaweed.

Serves 4

350 g (12½ oz) large flat mushrooms

250 g (8½ oz) queen scallops

200 g (7 oz) soba (Japanese buckwheat noodles)

125 g (4½ oz) Chinese leaves, shredded

170 g (6 oz) bean sprouts

4 spring onions, shredded

4 tbsp chopped fresh coriander

1 sheet toasted sushi nori, about 20 x 18 cm (8 x 7 in), cut into fine strips

Soy and garlic baste

2 garlic cloves, crushed

4 tbsp sunflower oil

2 tbsp soy sauce

2 tsp caster sugar

Soy dressing

juice of 1 large lemon

2 tsp finely grated fresh ginger

1 tbsp rich soy sauce

½ fresh red chilli, seeded and finely chopped

Preparation time: about 40 minutes

Each serving provides

kcal 414, **protein** 25 g, **fat** 14 g (of which saturated fat 2 g), **carbohydrate** 51 g (of which sugars 5 g), **fibre** 7 g

---

✓✓✓ B₁, B₆, B₁₂, C, E, folate, niacin, copper, selenium, zinc

---

✓✓ A, B₂, iron, potassium

---

1 Preheat the grill to high, and line the grill pan and a baking tray with foil. To make the baste, mix together the garlic, oil, soy sauce and sugar until smooth. Set aside one-third of the baste in a large mixing bowl. Brush some of the remaining baste over both sides of the mushrooms and place on the grill pan. Brush the scallops with the rest of the baste and place on the baking tray.

2 Bring a large saucepan of water to the boil and cook the soba for about 6 minutes, or according to the packet instructions, until tender. Drain.

3 While the noodles are cooking, make the dressing. Add the lemon juice, ginger, soy sauce and chilli to the reserved baste in the salad bowl and stir until smooth.

4 Add the drained noodles to the dressing and toss to coat. Add the Chinese leaves, bean sprouts, spring onions and coriander, and toss well again. Divide among 4 shallow bowls.

5 Grill the mushrooms for about 10 minutes or until tender, turning them over once. Remove from the heat, then grill the scallops for 2 minutes or until just cooked.

6 Slice the mushrooms and scatter them over the salad with any cooking juices. Add the scallops and the shreds of nori, and serve.

Another idea

● Make a prawn and rice noodle salad with coconut and ginger. For the dressing, mix together 1 tsp finely grated fresh root ginger, the juice of 1 lime, 4 tbsp coconut cream, 1 tbsp soy sauce, 1 tbsp chilli dipping sauce, 1 crushed garlic clove and 1 tsp caster sugar. Replace the soba with rice noodles, cooking them for 4–5 minutes or until just tender. Drain and toss with the dressing, then add 225 g (8 oz) halved cherry tomatoes, ½ cucumber, cut into strips, and 4 shredded spring onions. Grill 350 g (12½ oz) peeled raw tiger prawns until they turn pink, then toss into the salad while still warm, together with a handful of torn fresh basil leaves and 2 tbsp chopped fresh coriander.

Plus point

● Buckwheat, native to central Asia, was introduced to Europe at the end of the Middle Ages. It contains useful amounts of vitamin A and vitamins from the B group. It is low in fat and rich in starchy carbohydrate. Although buckwheat itself is gluten-free, buckwheat flour is usually mixed with wheat flour to make noodles such as soba, so this dish is not suitable for people with gluten or wheat intolerance.

special salads

119

Coronation chicken

Specially created for Queen Elizabeth's coronation lunch, this curry-flavoured salad with a fruity rice pilaf has become a traditional summer dish. Often made with cream and mayonnaise in the sauce, this updated version cuts the fat content by reducing the amount of mayonnaise and adding yogurt.

Serves 6

1 chicken, about 1.7 kg (3¾ lb), without giblets
1 onion, sliced
1 large carrot, coarsely chopped
1 celery stick, chopped
6 black peppercorns, lightly crushed
1 bay leaf
1 large banana
2 courgettes, cut into thin ribbons with a vegetable peeler
sprigs of fresh mint to garnish

Curry dressing

150 g (5½ oz) plain low-fat yogurt
4 tbsp mayonnaise
2 tbsp korma-flavoured curry paste
grated zest of 1 large lemon
1 tbsp lemon juice, or to taste
2 tbsp snipped fresh chives
2 tbsp chopped fresh mint
2 tbsp chopped parsley
salt and pepper

Raisin and mango pilaf

375 g (13 oz) basmati rice, well rinsed
45 g (1½ oz) raisins
45 g (1½ oz) ready-to-eat dried mango, chopped
75 g (2½ oz) pecan nuts

Preparation time: about 1½ hours, plus cooling

1 Place the chicken in a large saucepan and cover with water. Add the onion, carrot and celery, and bring almost to boiling point, skimming the surface as necessary. When bubbles begin to break through the surface, reduce the heat so the water is just simmering. Add the peppercorns and bay leaf, and simmer for 45 minutes or until the juices run clear from the chicken when you pierce the thigh.

2 Remove the chicken from the liquid and set aside to cool. Pour the cooking liquid through a fine sieve into a measuring jug. Discard the vegetables.

3 To make the pilaf, put the rice in a saucepan and add 600 ml (1 pint) of the strained cooking liquid. Stir in the raisins and mango. Bring to the boil, then reduce the heat, cover and simmer for 8–10 minutes, or according to the packet instructions, until all the liquid has been absorbed and the rice is tender.

4 Remove the rice from the heat and set aside, covered, for 5 minutes. Then transfer the rice to a bowl and leave to cool completely.

5 Meanwhile, make the dressing. Put the yogurt, mayonnaise, curry paste, and lemon zest and juice in a large mixing bowl and mix until well blended. Stir in the chives, mint and parsley and seasoning to taste.

6 When the chicken is completely cool, remove the skin and cut the meat into bite-sized pieces. Fold them into the curry dressing. (If you like, cover the chicken and chill; remove from the fridge 15 minutes before serving.) Slice the banana and gently stir it into the chicken mixture.

7 Stir the pecans into the rice pilaf and spoon onto 6 plates. Arrange the courgette ribbons on the pilaf and top with the chicken mixture. Garnish with fresh mint sprigs and serve.

Plus points

- Using the chicken stock to cook the rice ensures that none of the water-soluble vitamins that seeped into the water while the chicken was being poached are lost.
- Bananas are one of the best fruit sources of potassium, which is essential for muscle and nerve function and to help regulate blood pressure. Bananas also provide fibre, vitamins B_6 and C, magnesium and copper.

special salads

Each serving provides

kcal 618, **protein** 42 g, **fat** 21 g (of which saturated fat 3 g), **carbohydrate** 65 g (of which sugars 14 g), **fibre** 2 g

✓✓✓	B_1, B_6, E, niacin
✓✓	B_2, C, folate, copper, iron, potassium, selenium, zinc
✓	A, calcium

Some more ideas

• Use halved seedless green grapes instead of sliced banana.

• For a special occasion turkey coronation salad, buy 600 g (1 lb 5 oz) smoked turkey in one piece and cut into bite-sized pieces. To make the dressing, put 150 g (5½ oz) plain low-fat yogurt, 4 tbsp mayonnaise, 4 spring onions, the finely grated zest of 1 lemon and salt and pepper to taste in a blender or food processor and process until well blended. Transfer to a bowl and stir in the smoked turkey and sliced banana. Instead of the pilaf, cook 375 g (13 oz) mixed basmati and wild rice in boiling water for about 20 minutes or until tender. Drain and cool, then stir in 170 g (6 oz) finely shredded red cabbage and 85 g (3 oz) watercress, roughly chopped.

Avocado and prawn cups

Here, lettuce-lined salad bowls are filled with a mixture based on a popular combination – prawn and avocado – mixed with spiced new potatoes and topped with creamy bio yogurt for a real hot and cold taste explosion. Serve for lunch with brown or wholemeal bread.

Serves 4

600 g (1 lb 5 oz) new potatoes, scrubbed and diced
2 tbsp sunflower oil
1 small red onion, thinly sliced
1 garlic clove, crushed
1 fresh mild red chilli, seeded and finely chopped
1 tsp coriander seeds, roughly crushed
1 tsp cumin seeds, roughly crushed
1 large avocado
400 g (14 oz) peeled cooked prawns, thawed if frozen
juice of 2 limes
6 tbsp plain low-fat bio yogurt
3 tbsp chopped fresh coriander
8 round or iceberg lettuce leaves
salt and pepper

Preparation time: 25 minutes, plus cooling

1 Cook the potatoes in a saucepan of boiling water for 8 minutes or until just tender. Drain and refresh under cold running water. Dry in a clean tea-towel.

2 Heat the oil in a frying pan, add the onion and fry for 5 minutes or until softened and lightly browned. Add the garlic, chilli and crushed coriander and cumin seeds, and cook for 1 more minute, stirring. Stir in the potatoes and fry over a high heat for 3 minutes. Remove from the heat and leave to cool.

3 Peel the avocado, remove the stone and cut the flesh into cubes. Add to the potatoes together with the prawns and lime juice. Season with salt and pepper to taste, and toss gently.

4 Mix together the yogurt, chopped coriander and seasoning to taste. Arrange 2 lettuce leaves in each of 4 bowls. Spoon the salad into them and top with the coriander yogurt.

Some more ideas

• For an avocado, potato and tofu salad, replace the prawns with 250 g (8½ oz) plain tofu, drained and cubed. Add the tofu in step 2 with the garlic and spices.

• Use just 300 g (10½ oz) potatoes, and spoon the salad into 4 warmed round Arab flat breads or warmed chapattis. Top each with shredded lettuce and a spoonful of the yogurt and chopped coriander mixture.

Plus points

• Substances in avocados stimulate the production of collagen, which is why they have a reputation for being good for the skin.

• Bio yogurts are made using a strain of bacteria call bifida bacteria, and they have a milder, slightly creamier taste than ordinary yogurts. Bifida bacteria are believed to be more effective at keeping a healthy balance of bacteria in the gut than other yogurts. All types of yogurt are a good source of calcium (one 150 g pot provides about one-third of the recommended adult daily amount) along with phosphorus and vitamins B_2 and B_{12}. Although they don't always highlight the fact on the label, all yogurts bought from chiller cabinets are 'live', which means that they contain live bacteria.

Each serving provides

kcal 371, **protein** 28 g, **fat** 17 g (of which saturated fat 3 g), **carbohydrate** 29 g (of which sugars 6 g), **fibre** 4 g

✓✓✓	B_1, B_6, B_{12}, C, E, niacin
✓✓	B_2, folate, copper, potassium, selenium, zinc
✓	iron

special salads

123

Persian-style squash couscous

Wonderfully exotic and colourful, this vegetarian salad captures the flavours of ancient Persian cooking. Dates and sultanas are gently simmered with wine, spices and garlic, to flavour couscous, and then topped with roasted butternut and patty pan squashes, peppers and orange.

Serves 4

1 butternut squash, about 750 g (1 lb 10 oz), peeled

1 red pepper, halved and seeded

1 yellow pepper, halved and seeded

225 g (8 oz) baby patty pan squashes, halved if large

1 orange, unpeeled, cut into large chunks

4 bay leaves

1 cinnamon stick, halved

2 garlic cloves, chopped

2 tbsp extra virgin olive oil

½ tsp crushed dried chillies (optional)

Date and sultana couscous

1 tbsp extra virgin olive oil

1 onion, finely chopped

2 garlic cloves, chopped

75 g (2½ oz) stoned dates, chopped

75 g (2½ oz) sultanas

1 cinnamon stick, halved

2 cm (¾ in) piece fresh root ginger, finely chopped

150 ml (5 fl oz) dry white wine

250 g (8½ oz) couscous

1 can chickpeas, about 400 g, drained and rinsed

300 ml (10 fl oz) boiling water

2 tbsp chopped parsley

2 tbsp chopped fresh mint

juice of 1 orange

salt and pepper

Preparation time: about 1 hour

1 Preheat the oven to 200°C (400°F, gas mark 6). Cut the butternut squash in half lengthways, remove the seeds and cut across into thick slices. Cut each pepper half into 12 pieces. Put the squash and peppers in a roasting tin with the patty pans, orange, bay leaves, cinnamon stick and garlic. Drizzle over the olive oil and sprinkle with the dried chillies, if using. Roast for 25 minutes, turning once, until the vegetables are browned and tender.

2 Meanwhile, prepare the couscous. Heat the oil in a saucepan, add the onion and garlic, and fry for 5 minutes or until pale golden. Add the dates, sultanas, cinnamon, ginger and wine. Cover and cook gently for 5 minutes. Remove from the heat. Stir in the couscous and chickpeas, then add the boiling water. Cover and leave for 5 minutes.

3 Add the parsley, mint and orange juice to the couscous, and season with salt and pepper to taste. Mix and fluff up with a fork. Spoon onto 4 plates and top with the roasted vegetables. Serve warm or at room temperature.

Another idea

• For an aubergine and pearl barley salad, use 2 aubergines instead of the butternut squash, and roast with the peppers as in the main recipe. Instead of the date and sultana couscous, put 225 g (8 oz) pearl barley in a saucepan with 1 chopped onion, 1 halved cinnamon stick and 900 ml (1½ pints) vegetable or chicken stock. Bring to the boil, then cover and simmer for 1 hour or until the barley is just tender. Drain if necessary and cool, then toss with 85 g (3 oz) toasted walnut pieces, 1 tbsp chopped fresh mint, 1 tbsp chopped parsley, the grated zest and juice of 1 lemon and 1 tbsp extra virgin olive oil. Serve topped with the vegetables.

Plus point

• Dried dates are richer in potassium than fresh dates and contain more concentrated amounts of niacin, copper, iron and magnesium. Both dried dates and sultanas are a valuable source of soluble fibre.

Each serving provides Ⓥ

kcal 560, **protein** 16 g, **fat** 13 g (of which saturated fat 2 g), **carbohydrate** 101 g (of which sugars 40 g), **fibre** 12 g

✓✓✓	A, B₁, B₆, C, E, folate, niacin, iron
✓✓	calcium, potassium
✓	B₂, zinc

Sweet and sour duck salad

With ripe, juicy nectarines, red grapes, peppery green and red leaves, and slices of tender griddled duck, this is a particularly pretty salad. The unusual dressing complements and brings together all the ingredients.

Serves 4

250 g (8½ oz) mixed basmati and wild rice, well rinsed

450 g (1 lb) boneless duck breasts

2 tsp extra virgin olive oil

85 g (3 oz) watercress, tough stalks discarded

140 g (5 oz) seedless green grapes, halved

4 spring onions, thinly sliced

3 celery sticks, thinly sliced

4 nectarines

8 radicchio leaves or other red salad leaves

3 tbsp toasted pumpkin seeds

salt and pepper

Sweet and sour dressing

1 tsp grated fresh root ginger

1 small garlic clove, very finely chopped

1 tbsp sieved apricot jam

2 tsp raspberry vinegar or white wine vinegar

2 tbsp hazelnut oil

Preparation time: about 1 hour, plus cooling

Each serving provides

kcal 596, **protein** 33 g, **fat** 21 g (of which saturated fat 4 g), **carbohydrate** 70 g (of which sugars 18 g), **fibre** 3 g

✓✓✓ B$_1$, B$_2$, B$_6$, B$_{12}$, C, niacin, copper

✓✓ A, E, folate, iron, potassium, zinc

1 Cook the rice in a saucepan of boiling water for 20 minutes, or according to the packet instructions, until tender. Drain, then transfer to a bowl and allow to cool.

2 Heat a ridged cast-iron grill pan. Meanwhile, remove all the skin and fat from the duck breasts, and brush them on both sides with the olive oil. Place on the grill pan and cook over a moderately high heat for 3 minutes on each side (the meat will be rare, so cook longer if you prefer it well done). Allow the duck breasts to cool.

3 To make the dressing, put the ginger, garlic, apricot jam, vinegar and hazelnut oil in a small bowl and stir to combine. Season with salt to taste.

4 Chop half the watercress and add to the rice together with the grapes, spring onions and celery. Drizzle over half the dressing and mix gently.

5 Cut the duck breasts into thin slices. Thinly slice the nectarines. Arrange the radicchio and reserved watercress leaves on 4 plates and divide the rice salad among them. Arrange the duck and nectarine slices on top, drizzle over the remaining dressing and sprinkle with the pumpkin seeds.

Some more ideas

● Use ½ ripe Galia or Charentais melon, cut into thin crescents, instead of the nectarines.

● Make a griddled duck, sweet potato and apple salad. Cook 675 g (1½ lb) peeled and cubed sweet potatoes in enough boiling water to cover for 6–8 minutes or until tender. Drain well and cool slightly. For the dressing, stir 2½ tbsp each mayonnaise and plain low-fat yogurt with 1 tbsp Dijon mustard in a small bowl. Core and chop 1 large apple and toss with 2 tbsp lemon juice in a large mixing bowl. Add 3 celery sticks and 4 spring onions, all thinly sliced, and stir in the dressing. Fold in the sweet potatoes and the hot sliced duck. Serve warm, on a bed of mixed salad leaves.

Plus points

● Watercress, along with other dark green leafy vegetables, provides many vitamins and minerals including vitamin A (from beta-carotene), C and E, the B vitamins B$_6$, folate and niacin, and good amounts of calcium.

● Nectarines are high in vitamin C, fibre and beta-carotene (the darker the colour of the flesh, the higher the carotenoid content). They also offer B-complex vitamins.

● Radicchio, a member of the chicory family, has deep red and white tightly packed leaves. The red pigment means this vegetable is high in beta-carotene.

Summer chicken and pasta salad

Full of flavour and contrasting textures, the ingredients for this refreshing salad are mixed together in a smooth, creamy anchovy dressing. It's a good way to make the most of fresh broad beans (in season from the end of May to early July). At other times of the year, you can use frozen broad beans.

Serves 4

1 red pepper, quartered and seeded
1 yellow pepper, quartered and seeded
3 tbsp extra virgin olive oil
1 tbsp lemon juice
2 skinless boneless chicken breasts (fillets), about 340 g (12 oz) in total
1 can anchovy fillets, about 50 g, drained
2 tsp Dijon mustard
1 small garlic clove, crushed
2 tbsp Greek-style yogurt
2 tbsp warm water
1 red onion, thinly sliced
125 g (4½ oz) plump fresh asparagus spears
250 g (9 oz) fusilli (pasta spirals)
200 g (7 oz) podded fresh young broad beans
115 g (4 oz) mixed salad leaves
pepper

Preparation time: 1 hour, plus up to 12 hours chilling

Each serving provides

kcal 533, **protein** 35 g, **fat** 18 g (of which saturated fat 2 g), **carbohydrate** 61 g (of which sugars 10 g), **fibre** 8 g

✓✓✓	A, B$_1$, B$_6$, B$_{12}$, C, E, folate, niacin
✓✓	B$_2$, copper, potassium, zinc
✓	calcium, iron, selenium

1 Preheat the grill. Arrange the pepper quarters, skin side up, on the grill rack and grill for 5 minutes or until the skins are lightly charred. Turn the peppers over and grill for a further 2–3 minutes or until tender. Transfer to a polythene bag and leave until cool enough to handle, then peel off the skins and slice.

2 While the peppers are cooling, heat a ridged cast-iron grill pan or frying pan until very hot. Mix together 1½ tsp of the oil and 1 tsp of the lemon juice and brush it all over the chicken fillets. Add them to the pan, reduce the heat and cook for about 15 minutes, turning once, until the chicken is tender and cooked through; the juices should run clear when the thickest part is pierced with a knife.

3 Meanwhile, make the dressing. Put the anchovies in a blender with the remaining 2½ tbsp olive oil, 2 tsp lemon juice, the mustard, garlic, yogurt, water and pepper to taste. Blend until smooth and thick. Put the onion in a large bowl and pour over the dressing. Set aside.

4 When the chicken is cooked, remove it from the pan and set aside to cool. Add the asparagus to the pan and cook for 3–4 minutes, turning once, until tender. Remove from the pan and cut the spears in half. Set aside.

5 Cook the pasta in a large pan of boiling water for 10–12 minutes, or according to the packet instructions, until al dente. Add the broad beans for the last 3–4 minutes of cooking. Drain and rinse with cold water. Set aside.

6 Cut or tear the cooked chicken into strips. Add to the onions together with the pepper slices, asparagus, broad beans and pasta. Toss to coat everything with the dressing. Cover and chill for up to 12 hours. Remove from the fridge at least 15 minutes before serving, piled on a bed of salad leaves.

Plus points

• Anchovies contain calcium and phosphorus, both essential minerals for the maintenance of healthy bones and teeth. These minerals are retained in canned anchovy fillets.

• Serving a starchy carbohydrate like pasta with a small portion of low-fat protein in the form of lean meat, plus lots of vegetables, means this dish achieves a good, healthy balance from the different food groups.

special salads

Another idea

● Make a duck, penne and caramelised orange salad. Mix together the juice of ½ orange, 1 tsp light muscovado sugar, 2 tsp sunflower oil and 1 tbsp dark soy sauce. Pour it over 2 skinless boneless duck breasts, about 140 g (5 oz) each, and turn to coat, then leave to marinate for 30 minutes. Preheat the grill and cook the duck breasts for 10–15 minutes, turning once, until well browned (the inside will be pink). While the duck breasts are cooking, peel and thickly slice 3 large oranges. Sprinkle one side of the orange slices with 1 tbsp light muscovado sugar, and grill them alongside the duck for the last 5 minutes of the cooking time, until lightly browned. Instead of the fusilli in the main recipe, cook 250 g (8½ oz) penne. Slice the duck and put in a serving bowl with the oranges, penne and 115 g (4 oz) mixed salad leaves. For the dressing, whisk 2 tbsp sunflower oil with 2 tbsp orange juice and 2 tsp ginger juice (see step 3, Pork and pear salad with pecans, page 87). Season to taste. Pour over the salad, toss well and serve.

Mustardy beef fillet salad

Lean roasted fillet of beef makes a very special salad for entertaining. Here it is combined with new potatoes and green vegetables and tossed in a mustard-flavoured vinaigrette. Serve with French bread.

Serves 4

1 piece of beef fillet, from the tail end, about 450 g (1 lb)

1½ tsp extra virgin olive oil

340 g (12 oz) new potatoes, scrubbed

140 g (5 oz) thin green beans, halved

100 g (3½ oz) shelled fresh or frozen peas

85 g (3 oz) finely shredded leeks

2 tbsp snipped fresh chives

Mustard vinaigrette

3 tbsp extra virgin olive oil

1 tbsp red wine vinegar

1½ tsp Dijon mustard

pinch of caster sugar

salt and pepper

Preparation time: 35–40 minutes, plus cooling and chilling

Each serving provides

kcal 336, **protein** 28 g, **fat** 17 g (of which saturated fat 5 g), **carbohydrate** 17 g (of which sugars 4 g), **fibre** 3 g

✓✓✓	B_1, B_6, B_{12}, C, E, niacin, zinc
✓✓	B_2, folate, iron
✓	potassium, selenium

1 Preheat the oven to 230ºC (450ºF, gas mark 8). Rub the fillet with the olive oil and set on a rack in a roasting tin. Roast for 15 minutes for rare beef or up to 25 minutes for well done.

2 Meanwhile, whisk together the ingredients for the vinaigrette in a large mixing bowl.

3 Remove the beef from the oven and leave to stand for 5 minutes, then cut into thin slices against the grain. Add to the dressing and leave to cool.

4 Cook the potatoes in a saucepan of boiling water for 15 minutes or until tender. Drain well. When cool enough to handle, cut in half or into thick slices and add to the beef.

5 Drop the green beans into another pan of boiling water and cook for 1 minute. Add the peas and continue cooking for 3 minutes or until the vegetables are tender. Drain and refresh briefly under cold running water, then add to the beef and potatoes. Toss well. Cover and chill.

6 About 15 minutes before serving, remove the salad from the fridge and stir in the leeks and chives.

Another idea

• For a spicy pork fillet salad, mix 2 tbsp demerara sugar, 1 tsp celery salt, 1 tsp garlic granules, ½ tsp ground ginger, ½ tsp ground allspice, ½ tsp paprika and 1 tsp cider vinegar to make a thick, grainy paste. Spread this over 450 g (1 lb) pork fillet (tenderloin), then leave to marinate for up to 8 hours. Roast the pork in a preheated 200ºC (400ºF, gas mark 6) oven for 30 minutes or until cooked through. Remove from the oven and leave to cool. Meanwhile, rinse 250 g (8½ oz) basmati rice, then cook in a saucepan of boiling water for 10–12 minutes or until tender. Drain well and set aside to cool . To assemble the salad, cut the pork into cubes and mix with the rice and 100 g (3½ oz) fresh pineapple chunks, 1 large diced mango and 100 g (3½ oz) diced celery. Garnish with 2 tbsp chopped parsley and ½ tsp paprika.

Plus points

• Along with its many other nutritional benefits, beef is a useful source of vitamin D, which is found in relatively few foods. This vitamin is essential for the absorption of calcium, and thus helps in forming and maintaining healthy bones

• The pea was cultivated by the Greeks and Romans and was an important dried food in the Middle Ages. Fresh peas were not eaten in Europe until the 16th century, when they became a great delicacy and luxury. Peas supply good amounts of vitamins B_1, B_6 and niacin, along with dietary fibre, particularly the soluble variety. In addition, they provide useful amounts of folate and vitamin C.

special salads

Salads on the Side

Nutritious and delicious accompaniments

Tempting refreshing side salads can be made from an endless variety of ingredients – lettuces and other leaves, herbs, vegetables, fruit and even flowers. They'll boost the nutrients in any meal. Simple tossed salads can include myriad leaves, for exciting flavours; tomato salads can take advantage of the different colours and shapes in new varieties; and that family favourite, potato salad, can benefit from delicious baby new potatoes. Berries and luscious fruits like mango can be mixed into all kinds of salads, to add sweet flavour and vitamins. And crunchy salads can be made from cabbage, radishes and peanuts, or fennel, chicory and apple.

Tossed leaf and herb salad

A leafy salad with plenty of fresh herbs makes an excellent accompaniment to a whole range of dishes, from a simple roast chicken with potatoes, to pizza and pasta. For a crisp texture, make the salad just before you want to serve it and then toss with the dressing at the very last moment.

Serves 6

2 romaine or cos lettuces, cut across into thick slices

6 Lollo Rosso leaves

¼ cucumber, thinly sliced

12 large fresh basil leaves, roughly torn

1 tbsp coarsely chopped fresh tarragon

5 large spring onions, thinly sliced

6 tbsp Basic vinaigrette (see page 29)

Preparation time: 10 minutes

Each serving provides Ⓥ

kcal 132, **protein** 4 g, **fat** 10 g (of which saturated fat 1 g), **carbohydrate** 6 g (of which sugars 6 g), **fibre** 3 g

✓✓✓	B_1, B_6, C, E, folate, niacin
✓✓	A
✓	iron

1 Place the romaine or cos lettuce, Lollo Rosso, cucumber, herbs and spring onions in a large salad bowl.

2 Just before serving, drizzle over the dressing and toss thoroughly with salad servers or clean hands until the ingredients are coated lightly with the dressing. Serve immediately.

Some more ideas for tossed salads

● Add 30 g (1 oz) stoned green olives, whole or cut in half.

● For a green salad with a creamy avocado dressing, combine 2 Little Gem lettuces, separated into leaves, 40 g (1½ oz) each lamb's lettuce and watercress, 1 shredded courgette (or 3 thinly sliced dwarf courgettes), 4 sliced spring onions, 16 large fresh basil leaves and 40 g (1½ oz) stoned green olives. Make the dressing by blending or beating 1 large ripe avocado with 1 tbsp white wine vinegar, 3 tbsp extra virgin olive oil, 1 tsp Dijon mustard and seasoning to taste. Serve the avocado dressing on the side rather than mixed into the salad.

● Make a rocket and spinach salad with garlic croutons. For the croutons, toss 55 g (2 oz) cubed French bread with 1 tbsp extra virgin olive oil and 1 crushed garlic clove, then spread out on a baking tray. Bake in a preheated 180°C (350°F, gas mark 4) oven for 10 minutes or until golden. Make the dressing with 3 tbsp extra virgin olive oil, 2 tsp white wine vinegar, 1 tsp Dijon mustard, 1 tbsp capers, 2 finely chopped anchovy fillets, 1 finely chopped tomato and 8 chopped fresh basil leaves. Leave for a few minutes so the flavours can mingle. Put the croutons into a salad bowl with 1 romaine or cos lettuce, torn into pieces, 115 g (4 oz) baby spinach leaves and 45 g (1½ oz) rocket. Spoon over the dressing and serve.

● For a watercress and orange salad, mix the segments from 4 oranges with 85 g (3 oz) watercress, the leaves from 2 heads of chicory and 4 sliced shallots. For the dressing, whisk together 4 tbsp extra virgin olive oil, 2 tbsp white wine vinegar, 1 tbsp Acacia honey, seasoning to taste and a little Dijon mustard, if liked. Drizzle over the salad, toss and sprinkle with 4 tbsp lightly toasted pistachio nuts.

Plus points

● We would all benefit from eating at least 5 portions of fruit and vegetables a day, and salads can be a delicious and easy way to achieve this goal. A medium-sized helping of salad makes one portion.

● Lettuces such as romaine and cos are good sources of potassium and carotenoids. The darker outer leaves are more nutritious than the pale inner leaves.

Garlicky tomato salad

When tomatoes are at their peak of sweetness, this salad is particularly delicious. It's eye-catching too if you make it with a mixture of different-coloured tomatoes. New varieties are coming on the market all the time – look for yellow cherry tomatoes as well as small red or yellow pear-shaped plum tomatoes.

Serves 4

1 large soft lettuce, large leaves torn into smaller pieces

4 large or 6 small ripe plum tomatoes, about 500 g (1 lb 2 oz) in total, sliced

20 cherry tomatoes, about 225 g (8 oz) in total, halved

16 fresh basil leaves

1½ tbsp toasted pumpkin seeds

1½ tbsp toasted sunflower seeds

Garlic vinaigrette

1 small garlic clove, very finely chopped

1½ tsp red wine vinegar

2 tbsp extra virgin olive oil

salt and pepper

Preparation time: 15 minutes

1 To make the garlic vinaigrette, whisk together the garlic, vinegar, oil, and salt and pepper to taste in a small mixing bowl.

2 Place a layer of lettuce leaves on a serving platter or on 4 plates and arrange the sliced tomatoes and then the cherry tomatoes on top. Drizzle over the vinaigrette.

3 Scatter the basil leaves and the pumpkin and sunflower seeds over the tomatoes, and serve at once.

Some more ideas for tomato salads

• For a tomato and black olive salad, slice about 550 g (1¼ lb) ripe tomatoes, preferably beefsteak, and arrange on a serving platter. Top with 100 g (3½ oz) thinly sliced spring onions and drizzle over 1 tbsp extra virgin olive oil and the juice of ¼ lemon. Arrange 8 black olives, halved and stoned, on top and sprinkle with 2 tbsp chopped parsley.

• Make a salad of fresh and sun-dried tomatoes. Cut 6 ripe plum tomatoes into thin wedges and put them in a mixing bowl. Thinly slice 3 sun-dried tomatoes and add to the bowl. Make a vinaigrette by whisking 1½ tbsp of the oil from the jar of sun-dried tomatoes with 1½ tsp wine vinegar and seasoning to taste. Drizzle over the tomatoes and marinate briefly. Arrange 100 g (3½ oz) rocket on 4 plates and divide the tomatoes among them. Sprinkle with 2 tbsp toasted pine nuts and serve.

• Try a salad of cherry tomatoes and sugarsnap peas. Trim 250 g (8½ oz) sugarsnap peas and steam for about 3 minutes or until tender but still crisp. Refresh under cold running water, then cool. Mix with 375 g (13 oz) cherry tomatoes, halved if large, and 6 thinly sliced spring onions. Make the garlic vinaigrette as in the main recipe and drizzle it over the tomatoes and peas. Add 3 tbsp chopped fresh mint, or 1 tbsp each chopped fresh tarragon and parsley, and toss to mix.

Plus points

• Pumpkin seeds are one of the richest vegetarian sources of zinc, a mineral that is essential for the functioning of the immune system and for growth and wound healing. They are a good source of protein and unsaturated fat and a useful source of iron, magnesium and fibre.

• Tomatoes are a rich source of vitamin C, an important nutrient for maintaining immunity and healthy skin. The vitamin C is concentrated in the jellylike substance surrounding the seeds.

Each serving provides   ⓥ

kcal 160, **protein** 5 g, **fat** 12 g (of which saturated fat 2 g), **carbohydrate** 9 g (of which sugars 7 g), **fibre** 3 g

✓✓✓	A, B₁, B₆, C, E, niacin
✓✓	folate, copper
✓	iron, zinc

Mixed salad leaves with flowers and blueberries

This pretty summer salad is a delightful combination of edible flowers, salad leaves, alfalfa sprouts and juicy fresh blueberries. Some large supermarkets sell packs of edible flowers. Or you can pick them from your garden – just be sure to choose those that have not been sprayed with pesticides.

Serves 4

1 small Oak Leaf lettuce, torn into bite-sized pieces

85 g (3 oz) rocket

85 g (3 oz) alfalfa sprouts

100 g (3½ oz) blueberries

30 g (1 oz) mixed edible flowers, including some or all of the following: nasturtiums, borage, violas or pansies, and herb flowers such as sage and rosemary

Honey mustard dressing

3 tbsp grapeseed oil

juice of 1 small lemon

1 tsp Dijon mustard

1 tsp clear honey

salt and pepper

Preparation time: 10–15 minutes

Each serving provides Ⓥ

kcal 107, **protein** 2 g, **fat** 9 g (of which saturated fat 1 g), **carbohydrate** 5 g (of which sugars 5 g), **fibre** 2 g

✓✓✓	B₁, B₆, C, niacin
✓✓	E
✓	A, folate

1 To make the dressing, whisk the oil with the lemon juice, mustard, honey, and salt and pepper to taste in a large shallow salad bowl.

2 Add the lettuce and rocket and toss to coat with the dressing. Sprinkle the salad with the alfalfa sprouts and blueberries. Arrange the flowers on top and serve at once.

Some more ideas for flowery salads

• Make a flowery carrot salad. Tear 1 batavia or Oak Leaf lettuce into bite-sized pieces and put into a shallow salad bowl. Add 2 carrots, cut into long thin ribbons with a swivel vegetable peeler, 2 oranges, peeled and divided into segments, and 75 g (2½ oz) blueberries. Make the honey mustard dressing as in the main recipe, using orange juice instead of lemon. Drizzle it over the salad and garnish with mixed orange and yellow nasturtium flowers.

• For a refreshingly lemony leaf and raspberry salad, mix 15 g (½ oz) sweet cicely leaves and a few lemon geranium leaves with 1 small Webb's Wonder or cos lettuce, torn into pieces. Scatter over 100 g (3½ oz) raspberries. For the dressing, whisk 2 tbsp extra virgin olive oil with the juice of 1 lemon and seasoning to taste. Garnish the salad with 30 g (1 oz) mixed chive, sweet cicely and mint or viola flowers.

• Try a peppery salad with pears and wild garlic. Separate 2 Little Gem lettuces into leaves and mix with 85 g (3 oz) rocket in a salad bowl. For the dressing whisk 3 tbsp extra virgin olive oil with the juice of 1 lemon and 3 tbsp chopped fresh chives. Add 1 ripe red Williams pear, cored and thinly sliced, and turn to coat with the dressing, then add the pear and dressing to the salad leaves and toss gently. Garnish with 30 g (1 oz) mixed wild garlic, chive and borage flowers.

Plus points

• Naturally sweet blueberries are rich in vitamin C and also contain antibacterial compounds thought to be effective against some gastro-intestinal disorders and urinary infections such as cystitis.

• The nutritional value of petals and flower heads is very small as they are used in such tiny quantities, but you will get some essential oils and phytochemicals, particularly antioxidants, from some flowers, especially herb flowers.

New potato salad

A potato salad with a creamy dressing is always a winner, and the version here, with cucumber, spring onions and fresh herbs, is sure to become a firm favourite with your family. Potatoes are full of goodness, particularly if the skins are left on, so this side salad will make a nutritious addition to any meal.

Serves 4

900 g (2 lb) tiny new potatoes, scrubbed

2 tbsp dry white vermouth or dry white wine

dash of white wine vinegar, or to taste

1 garlic clove, finely chopped

3 tbsp mayonnaise

5 tbsp plain low-fat yogurt

½ large firm cucumber, diced

75 g (2½ oz) spring onions, thinly sliced

3 tbsp chopped fresh dill

1½ tbsp chopped fresh tarragon

salt and pepper

fresh dill and tarragon leaves to garnish

Preparation time: about 40 minutes

1 Cook the potatoes in a saucepan of boiling water for about 10 minutes or until they are just tender. Drain and return them to the pan. Set over a low heat and shake them around for a few minutes to evaporate any moisture. Transfer the potatoes to a mixing bowl and leave to cool for about 5 minutes.

2 Sprinkle the vermouth or wine and wine vinegar over the potatoes. Season with salt and pepper to taste. Turn the potatoes to mix, then leave to cool completely.

3 Meanwhile, mix together the garlic, mayonnaise and yogurt in a small bowl until smooth.

4 When the potatoes are cool, add the cucumber, spring onions, dill and tarragon. Spoon on the mayonnaise and yogurt mixture, and stir gently to mix everything together. Serve at cool room temperature or chilled, garnished with dill and tarragon leaves.

Plus points

● Using fresh herbs in a salad helps to reduce the need for salt. Our taste for salt and salty foods is something we learn to like the more we eat. If you gradually reduce the amount of salt you use, your palate will adapt as the salt receptors on the tongue become much more sensitive to salt. The process takes about 4 weeks.

● Herbalists use dill to help relieve stomach cramps, flatulence and heartburn.

Some more ideas for potato salads

● For a new potato salad with peas and beans to serve 4–6, cook the potatoes for 6 minutes, then add 75 g (2½ oz) each of shelled fresh young peas, or frozen petits pois, shelled fresh young broad beans, or frozen broad beans, and chopped green beans. Cook for a further 5 minutes, then drain and refresh under cold running water. Pat dry in a clean tea-towel, then transfer to a bowl and sprinkle over 2 tbsp dry white vermouth or dry white wine. Combine 1 small red onion, finely chopped, 2 chopped garlic cloves, 2 tbsp chopped fresh flat-leaf parsley, 2 tbsp mild French mustard, 2 tbsp extra virgin olive oil, 1 tbsp white wine vinegar and seasoning to taste. Pour this dressing over the potatoes and vegetables and mix well. Eat the salad warm or cold.

Each serving provides

kcal 263, **protein** 6 g, **fat** 10 g (of which saturated fat 2 g), **carbohydrate** 40 g (of which sugars 6 g), **fibre** 3 g

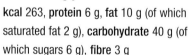

✓✓✓	B₁, B₆, C, E, niacin
✓✓	folate, potassium
✓	copper

salads on the side

• Make a piquant potato, pickled cucumber and apple salad. Cook 600 g (1 lb 5 oz) large potatoes, peeled and cut into thick slices, in boiling water for 10 minutes or until just tender (do not let them become mushy). Drain and return to the pan. Sprinkle with 2 tbsp dry white vermouth or dry white wine and warm over a low heat for 1–2 minutes to evaporate the alcohol. Leave to cool for about 10 minutes or until cool enough to handle, then cut into large dice and transfer to a bowl. Add 50 g (1¾ oz) diced pickled cucumber, 5 spring onions, thinly sliced, 1 small apple, chopped, and 1 chopped celery stick, and toss gently to mix. Warm 1 tbsp clear honey until it is runny, then mix it with 4 tbsp cider vinegar and 1 tsp mild French mustard. Stir this dressing into the potato mixture, together with 3 tbsp soured cream. Cover and chill. Just before serving, garnish with 2 small cooked beetroot (not vinegared), cut into small dice.

Avocado salad with raspberries

It's a misconception that avocados cannot be enjoyed in a healthy diet because of their high fat content. Yes, they do contain a great deal of fat, but it is the good monounsaturated type. In this salad, the creaminess of avocado is complemented by fresh raspberries and a fruity vinaigrette.

Serves 4

2 avocados

170 g (6 oz) mixed salad leaves, such as frisée, baby chard and lamb's lettuce

100 g (3½ oz) raspberries

sprigs of fresh mint to garnish

Raspberry vinaigrette

2 tbsp extra virgin olive oil

1½ tbsp raspberry vinegar

1 tbsp single cream

finely grated zest of ½ orange

½ tsp orange juice

pinch of caster sugar

salt and pepper

Preparation time: about 10 minutes

Each serving provides Ⓥ

kcal 255, **protein** 3 g, **fat** 25 g (of which saturated fat 5 g), **carbohydrate** 4 g (of which sugars 3 g), **fibre** 4 g

✓✓✓	B₁, B₆, C, E, niacin
✓	B₂, folate, copper, potassium

1 Put all the ingredients for the raspberry vinaigrette in a large salad bowl, adding salt and pepper to taste, and whisk to mix.

2 Halve the avocados and remove the stone, then peel and dice the flesh. Drop immediately into the dressing and turn to coat, to prevent the avocado from turning brown.

3 Add the salad leaves to the bowl and toss gently with the avocado. Scatter over the raspberries and garnish with mint sprigs. Serve at once.

Some more ideas for avocado salads

• For an Italian-style avocado and mozzarella starter salad, thickly slice each avocado half horizontally and arrange on 4 plates with 140 g (5 oz) sliced mozzarella cheese. Sprinkle with 100 g (3½ oz) sliced sun-dried tomatoes, then drizzle 1 tbsp extra virgin olive oil, or oil from the jar of tomatoes, over each serving. Season with pepper and garnish with fresh basil leaves.

• For an avocado and grapefruit salad, make the vinaigrette as in the main recipe, but replace the raspberry vinegar with pink grapefruit juice and omit the orange juice. Use watercress or rocket, or a mixture of watercress and baby spinach leaves, instead of mixed salad leaves, and 1 large pink grapefruit, peeled, divided into segments and each segment cut in half, instead of raspberries. Toss the grapefruit with the avocado and leaves.

• Make a tropical avocado and mango salad. Line 4 plates with cos or romaine lettuce leaves. Cut each avocado half horizontally into thin slices and arrange on the plates with 1 thinly sliced, large ripe mango. Scatter 3 chopped spring onions over the top. Drizzle each salad with 1 tbsp extra virgin olive oil and 1–2 tbsp orange juice, and dust lightly with cayenne pepper.

Plus points

• Avocados are high in oleic acid, which helps to lower levels of the 'bad' LDL cholesterol while raising levels of the 'good' HDL cholesterol. Just one avocado provides half the recommended daily intake of vitamin B₆. They also provide useful amounts of vitamin E and potassium.

• Raspberries are an excellent source of vitamin C and also provide useful amounts of vitamin E.

salads on the side

Beetroot with horseradish cream dressing

With a vibrant, deep ruby-red colour and a fresh flavour and texture, raw beetroot is completely different from beetroot pickled in malt vinegar. It makes a spectacular and nutritious salad.

Serves 4

675 g (1½ lb) raw beetroot, peeled

1 small red onion, finely chopped

1 tbsp sunflower oil

2 tbsp orange juice

2 tsp red wine vinegar

150 g (5½ oz) small salad leaves, such as beetroot tops, baby chard, lamb's lettuce, red mustard, mizuna, baby spinach or sorrel

Horseradish dressing

3 tbsp soured cream

3 tbsp plain low-fat yogurt

1 tsp grated fresh horseradish or 2 tsp horseradish sauce

2 tbsp chopped fresh dill

salt and pepper

Preparation time: 20 minutes, plus 30 minutes marinating

Each serving provides Ⓥ

kcal 181, **protein** 5 g, **fat** 10 g (of which saturated fat 3 g), **carbohydrate** 18 g (of which sugars 16 g), **fibre** 4 g

✓✓✓	B$_1$, B$_6$, C, E, folate, niacin
✓	A, calcium

---

1 Grate the beetroot into a mixing bowl, keeping all the juices (this can also be done in a food processor with a coarse grating disc). Add the onion and stir to mix with the beetroot.

2 Whisk together the oil, orange juice and vinegar in a small bowl. Season with salt and pepper to taste. Pour over the beetroot and onion and toss well. Cover and leave to marinate at room temperature for 30 minutes. (The salad can be prepared up to this stage and kept for up to 24 hours in the fridge.)

3 Put the salad leaves in a serving bowl. Add the marinated beetroot and onion and toss together.

4 For the dressing, stir the soured cream, yogurt, horseradish and dill together. Spoon the dressing on the salad and serve immediately.

Some more ideas for beetroot salads

• For a beetroot, carrot and orange salad, first soak 55 g (2 oz) raisins in 3 tbsp orange juice for at least 1 hour. Cut 225 g (8 oz) peeled raw beetroot and 225 g (8 oz) carrots into fine matchstick strips. Gently heat 2 tbsp sunflower oil with 1 tsp caraway seeds in a small pan for 1 minute. Remove from the heat and whisk in 2 tsp lime juice. Pour over the raw vegetables, toss together and leave to cool. Meanwhile, peel and slice 4 oranges, and arrange on a serving platter with 75 g (2½ oz) watercress sprigs. Spoon the beetroot and carrots into the middle and scatter over the soaked raisins and 15 g (½ oz) toasted sunflower seeds.

• For a beetroot slaw, grate 340 g (12 oz) peeled raw beetroot and mix with 225 g (8 oz) finely shredded red cabbage and 1 thinly sliced red onion. For the dressing, mix ¼ tsp mustard powder with 1 tbsp clear honey, then whisk in 1 tbsp orange juice, 1 tsp red wine vinegar, ¼ tsp paprika and seasoning to taste. Pour over the vegetables, toss well and leave to marinate for 30 minutes.

Plus point

• In Chinese medicine, beetroot is said to strengthen the heart, sedate the spirit, purify the blood and treat a sluggish liver. Eaten raw or cooked, beetroot is a good source of folate and provides some iron; when pickled, most of the folate is destroyed. For some people, eating beetroot can cause their urine to turn pink. This is no cause for alarm, it simply indicates a genetically inherited inability to metabolise betacyanin, the red pigment that gives beetroot its characteristic colour. This harmless compound simply passes through the digestive system unchanged.

Sprouted bean salad

The nutritional content of pulses and grains increases dramatically when they are sprouted – there is 60% more vitamin C and almost 30% more B vitamins in the sprout than in the original seed. Choose fresh-looking, crisp sprouts, preferably with the seed still attached. They will keep for up to 2 days in a plastic bag in the fridge.

Serves 4

55 g (2 oz) dried apricots, chopped

125 g (4½ oz) dried mango, chopped

4 tbsp apple juice

2 courgettes, cut into 1 cm (½ in) dice

2 small heads chicory, halved lengthways and sliced across

300 g (10½ oz) assorted bean and grain sprouts, such as mung, aduki and alfalfa

Dressing

30 g (1 oz) fresh root ginger, peeled and finely chopped

1 tsp wholegrain mustard

2 tsp cider vinegar

2 tsp clear honey

3 tbsp sunflower oil

1 tbsp poppy seeds

salt and pepper

Preparation time: 25 minutes, plus 1 hour soaking

Each serving provides Ⓥ

kcal 211, **protein** 6 g, **fat** 11 g (of which saturated fat 1 g), **carbohydrate** 28 g (of which sugars 26 g), **fibre** 5 g

✓✓✓	B₁, B₆, E, niacin
✓✓	C, copper, iron, potassium
✓	A, calcium, zinc

1 Put the dried apricots and mango in a salad bowl and spoon over the apple juice. Cover and leave to soak for 1 hour or until the juice has been soaked up and the fruit is plump.

2 Add the courgettes, chicory, and bean and grain sprouts, and toss together to mix thoroughly.

3 To make the dressing, first press the ginger in a garlic press until you have 2 tsp of ginger juice. Then whisk this juice with the mustard, vinegar, honey and salt and pepper to taste. Gradually add the oil, whisking until slightly thickened. Stir in the poppy seeds. Pour the dressing over the salad, toss and serve at once.

Some more ideas for sprout salads

• Many supermarkets sell bags of mixed sprouted beans, grains and seeds, but it is very easy to grow them at home. The most suitable for salads are alfalfa, mung and aduki beans and fenugreek. Rinse the beans or seeds, then place in a large jar. Fill the jar with water, then cover with a piece of muslin secured with an elastic band. Leave to soak in a warm place overnight. The next day, pour off the water through the muslin, then refill the jar with water through the muslin. Shake gently, then drain the water thoroughly and leave the jar on its side, away from direct sunlight. Repeat this process in the morning and evening for 2–3 days until sprouted. Place the jar in a sunny but not too hot place for a few days, still rinsing regularly, until the sprouts have grown to the desired size. Rinse well and remove any ungerminated beans or seeds before using.

• For a sprouted bean salad with fresh apricots and orange, mix together 2 chopped celery sticks, 1 thinly sliced bulb of fennel, 115 g (4 oz) quartered red radishes, 2 oranges, peeled and divided into segments, 4 stoned and sliced apricots, and 115 g (4 oz) alfalfa sprouts. For the dressing, whisk 2 tbsp sunflower oil with 2 tbsp orange juice and 1 tsp lemon juice. Season to taste. Pour over the salad and toss.

Plus points

• Naturopaths believe that cider vinegar has therapeutic properties, suggesting that 1–2 tsp taken in a glass of water 2–3 times a day can help to relieve the symptoms of arthritis.

• Dried fruit is a concentrated source of nutrients, including iron, calcium, phosphorus and some B vitamins. It is also a great provider of dietary fibre.

• Although only a small quantity is used in this recipe, poppy seeds make a contribution to the protein content of this salad.

Baby leeks with tarragon

Here, young tender leeks are marinated in a piquant tarragon vinaigrette and then sprinkled with hard-boiled egg and crispy crumbs. This makes an excellent side salad or starter, or a light lunch for 2 with crusty bread. For the best flavour, serve the salad at cool room temperature, not chilled.

Serves 4

15 g (½ oz) coarse Granary or white
 breadcrumbs
2 eggs
550 g (1¼ lb) baby leeks, halved lengthways

Tarragon vinaigrette

3 tbsp groundnut oil
2 tsp white wine vinegar
1 tsp Dijon mustard
1 tsp chopped fresh tarragon
salt and pepper

Preparation time: 25 minutes

1 Preheat the grill to high. Spread out the breadcrumbs on a sheet of foil, then toast under the grill for about 4 minutes or until golden and crunchy.

2 Bring a saucepan of water to the boil. Add the eggs and cook for 10 minutes. At the same time, steam the leeks for 5–8 minutes or until just tender. (The leeks can be steamed over the eggs.)

3 Meanwhile, whisk together the ingredients for the tarragon vinaigrette and season with salt and pepper to taste.

4 Drain the hard-boiled eggs and cool under cold running water, then shell and finely chop them.

5 Arrange the leeks on a platter or individual serving plates and drizzle over the vinaigrette. Leave to cool, then scatter over the egg and breadcrumbs. Serve before the crumbs lose their texture in the dressing.

Some more ideas for marinated salads

• For a marinated asparagus salad with Parmesan, steam 500 g (1 lb 2 oz) asparagus spears for 10–12 minutes or until just tender. Make the dressing with 4 tbsp extra virgin olive oil, 1 tbsp balsamic vinegar, 1 crushed garlic clove and seasoning to taste. Spoon it over the warm asparagus and cool, then scatter over 30 g (1 oz) Parmesan cheese shavings.

• For marinated fennel with orange vinaigrette, cut 2 large bulbs of fennel, about 500 g (1 lb 2 oz) in total, into quarters lengthways and steam for 10–12 minutes or until just tender. Make the dressing with the grated zest of ½ orange, the juice of 1 orange, 1 tsp balsamic vinegar, 1 tbsp lemon juice, 3 tbsp extra virgin olive oil and seasoning to taste. Spoon it over the fennel and cool, then scatter over 2 tbsp toasted pine nuts.

• For a marinated broccoli and cauliflower salad, steam 250 g (8½ oz) each broccoli and cauliflower florets for 10 minutes or until tender. Meanwhile, whisk 3 tbsp extra virgin olive oil with 1 tsp Dijon mustard, 2 tsp red wine vinegar, 2 tbsp chopped fresh basil, 1 tbsp snipped fresh chives, a pinch of caster sugar and seasoning to taste in a bowl. Toss the vegetables in the dressing and leave to cool.

Plus point

• A member of the onion family, leeks are a useful source of vitamin C, folate and phytochemicals that can help to fight infection and prevent disease. The green part of leeks is a good source of beta-carotene.

Each serving provides	Ⓥ
kcal 161, **protein** 6 g, **fat** 12 g (of which saturated fat 3 g), **carbohydrate** 6 g (of which sugars 3 g), **fibre** 3 g	
✓✓✓ B₁, B₆, B₁₂, C, E, niacin	
✓✓ A, folate	
✓ B₂, iron	

Roasted pepper salad

This colourful salad makes a tasty accompaniment to seafood, chicken or lamb, or it can be served as part of a Mediterranean starter selection, with ciabatta bread or baguette. Peppers are an excellent source of vitamin C, and when roasted they still retain substantial amounts of this important vitamin.

Serves 6

2 large red peppers
2 large yellow or orange peppers
2 large green peppers
2½ tbsp extra virgin olive oil
2 tsp balsamic vinegar
1 small garlic clove, very finely chopped or crushed
salt and pepper

To garnish
12 black olives, stoned
a handful of small fresh basil leaves

Preparation time: 45 minutes, plus cooling

1 Preheat the oven to 200°C (400°F, gas mark 6). Brush the peppers with 1 tbsp of the olive oil and arrange them in a shallow roasting tin. Roast for about 35 minutes or until the pepper skins are evenly darkened, turning them 3 or 4 times. Place the peppers in a polythene bag and leave until they are cool enough to handle.

2 Working over a bowl to catch the juice, peel the peppers. Cut them in half and discard the cores and seeds (strain out any seeds that fall into the juice), then cut into thick slices.

3 Measure 1½ tbsp of the pepper juice into a small bowl (discard the remainder). Add the vinegar, garlic and salt and pepper to taste, and whisk in the remaining 1½ tbsp olive oil.

4 Arrange the peppers on a serving platter or on individual salad plates. Drizzle over the dressing and garnish with the olives and basil leaves.

Some more ideas for pepper salads

• For a roasted red pepper and onion salad to serve 4, quarter and seed 4 red peppers and put them in a baking dish with 4 small red onions, quartered. Drizzle over 1½ tbsp extra virgin olive oil and season to taste. Roast in a preheated 200°C (400°F, gas mark 6) oven for about 35 minutes, turning once, until the vegetables are tender and browned around the edges. Cool, then peel the peppers, if wished, holding them over the baking dish. Whisk 2 tsp lemon juice with 1½ tbsp extra virgin olive oil in a salad bowl and season to taste. Add 115 g (4 oz) rocket or mixed red salad leaves and toss to coat. Pile the peppers and onions on top and drizzle over their cooking juices.

• For an Oriental-style pepper and Chinese leaf salad to serve 4, seed and thinly slice 2 red peppers (or 1 red and 1 yellow pepper) and 1 fresh red chilli. Mix in a salad bowl with 150 g (5½ oz) shredded Chinese leaves. For the dressing, whisk together 1 tbsp rice vinegar, 1 tsp toasted sesame oil, 2 tsp groundnut oil and 1 tsp soy sauce. Drizzle over the vegetables and toss to coat. Sprinkle with 2 tbsp toasted sesame seeds and serve.

Plus points

• Herbalists recommend basil as a natural tranquiliser. It is also believed to aid digestion, ease stomach cramps and help relieve the headaches associated with colds.

• Olives are a source of vitamin E, although they are usually not eaten in large enough quantities to make a significant contribution to the diet.

Each serving provides

kcal 97, **protein** 2 g, **fat** 6 g (of which saturated fat 1 g), **carbohydrate** 10 g (of which sugars 9 g), **fibre** 3 g

✓✓✓ A, B₁, B₆, C, E, niacin

✓✓ folate

150

Apple and fennel with blue cheese dressing

This is a tasty salad to have in your repertoire for the winter months when salad leaves and tomatoes are not at their best. Bulb fennel has a distinctive, sweet aniseed flavour that works well with bitter chicory and refreshing crisp apple. A creamy blue cheese dressing is the perfect partner.

Serves 4

30 g (1 oz) shelled hazelnuts

1 large bulb of fennel, thinly sliced

1 large head of chicory, cut across into shreds

2 red-skinned dessert apples

100 g (3½ oz) radicchio leaves

2 tbsp snipped fresh chives

Blue cheese dressing

55 g (2 oz) blue cheese, such as Danish Blue, crumbled

2 tbsp tepid water

6 tbsp plain low-fat bio yogurt

pepper

Preparation time: about 20 minutes

1 To make the dressing, put the blue cheese in a bowl with the water and mash to a smooth paste using the back of a spoon. Stir in the yogurt to make a thick, fairly smooth dressing. Season to taste with pepper. Set aside.

2 Heat a small non-stick frying pan over a high heat. Add the hazelnuts and toast for about 2 minutes or until they smell nutty, stirring frequently. Immediately tip onto a clean tea-towel and rub to remove the papery outer skins. Coarsely chop the nuts.

3 Add the fennel and chicory to the dressing and stir to combine. Core the apples and cut into very thin slices, then add to the salad. Toss gently, making sure the apples are coated in dressing. Fold in the hazelnuts.

4 Arrange the radicchio leaves on 4 plates. Top with the salad and sprinkle with the chives. Serve at once.

Another idea

● For a Cheddar cheese and apple salad, make the dressing by mixing 100 g (3½ oz) finely grated mature Cheddar cheese with 6 tbsp plain low-fat bio yogurt or reduced-fat crème fraîche (it will not be completely smooth). Core and chop 2 red apples and 2 green apples, and stir them into the dressing together with 2 thinly sliced celery sticks and 2 tbsp chopped parsley. Season to taste. Arrange 150 g (5½ oz) mixed salad leaves and 85 g (3 oz) watercress on 4 plates, and top with the cheese and apple salad. Serve immediately, as a light main dish.

Plus points

● Chicory is native to India but was known to the Greeks and Romans. It is a useful source of vitamin C, beta-carotene and potassium. It is widely used in herbal medicine – as an appetite stimulant, to stimulate the liver and gall bladder, and to treat urinary tract infections.

● Apples provide good amounts of potassium and soluble fibre in the form of pectin. Eating apples can benefit the teeth too, helping to prevent gum disease.

Each serving provides Ⓥ

kcal 141, protein 5 g, fat 10 g (of which saturated fat 3 g), carbohydrate 10 g (of which sugars 8 g), fibre 4 g

✓✓✓	B₁, B₆, E, niacin
✓✓	C, folate
✓	A, calcium, copper

Crunchy nut coleslaw

Everyone loves coleslaw, and this fresh-tasting version will be sure to appeal to the whole family. Made with white cabbage, carrot and radishes, it is flecked with spring onions, sweet sultanas and roasted peanuts, and tossed with a creamy dressing that is healthily low in fat.

Serves 4

200 g (7 oz) white cabbage, finely shredded

1 large carrot, about 150 g (5½ oz), coarsely grated

50 g (1¾ oz) sultanas

4 spring onions, finely chopped, with the white and green parts kept separate

2 tbsp mayonnaise

150 g (5½ oz) plain low-fat yogurt

30 g (1 oz) radishes, sliced

50 g (1¾ oz) unsalted roasted peanuts

3 tbsp chopped parsley or snipped fresh chives, or a mixture of the two (optional)

salt and pepper

Preparation time: 15 minutes

1 Mix together the cabbage, carrot, sultanas and white parts of the spring onion in a large bowl.

2 Stir the mayonnaise and yogurt together and season with salt and pepper to taste. Stir this dressing into the cabbage mixture and toss to coat all the ingredients.

3 Just before serving, stir in the radishes and peanuts, and sprinkle with the chopped green parts of the spring onions and the parsley or chives.

Some more ideas for coleslaw

• Toss 1 cored and diced red-skinned dessert apple with 2 tbsp lemon juice, then stir into the coleslaw with 1 tsp caraway seeds.

• Add 100 g (3½ oz) canned or thawed frozen sweetcorn.

• Lightly toast 1 tbsp pumpkin seeds and 2 tbsp sunflower seeds under the grill and use to garnish the coleslaw in place of the herbs.

• For a celeriac coleslaw, use 250 g (8½ oz) peeled celeriac, cut into matchstick strips, instead of white cabbage. Flavour the yogurt and mayonnaise dressing with 2 tsp wholegrain mustard, or 1 tsp Dijon mustard and 1 tbsp mango chutney.

• For a red cabbage and blue cheese coleslaw to serve 4–6, mix together 200 g (7 oz) finely shredded red cabbage with 150 g (5½ oz) tiny cauliflower florets, 150 g (5½ oz) grated carrot, ½ finely chopped red onion and 50 g (1¾ oz) dried cranberries or cherries. Make the dressing by mashing 150 g (5½ oz) plain low-fat yogurt with 115 g (4 oz) crumbled St Agur cheese and seasoning to taste. Garnish with 2 rashers of lean back bacon, derinded, grilled until crisp and cut into thin strips.

Each serving provides

kcal 209, **protein** 7 g, **fat** 12 g (of which saturated fat 2 g), **carbohydrate** 19 g (of which sugars 18 g), **fibre** 3 g

✓✓✓	A, B₁, B₆, C, E, niacin
✓✓	folate
✓	calcium, copper, potassium

Plus points

• Roasted peanuts are a delicious and nutritious addition to this recipe. New research suggests that a daily intake of peanuts, peanut butter or peanut (groundnut) oil may help to lower total cholesterol, harmful LDL cholesterol and triglyceride levels and thus help to protect against coronary heart disease.

• Home-made coleslaw not only looks and tastes far superior to shop-bought coleslaw, but it will be much lower in fat.

A glossary of nutritional terms

Antioxidants These are compounds that help to protect the body's cells against the damaging effects of free radicals. Vitamins C and E, beta-carotene (the plant form of vitamin A) and the mineral selenium, together with many of the phytochemicals found in fruit and vegetables, all act as antioxidants.

Calorie A unit used to measure the energy value of food and the intake and use of energy by the body. The scientific definition of 1 calorie is the amount of heat required to raise the temperature of 1 gram of water by 1 degree Centigrade. This is such a small amount that in this country we tend to use the term kilocalories (abbreviated to *kcal*), which is equivalent to 1000 calories. Energy values can also be measured in kilojoules (kJ): 1 kcal = 4.2 kJ.

A person's energy (calorie) requirement varies depending on his or her age, sex and level of activity. The estimated average daily energy requirements are:

Age (years)	Female (kcal)	Male (kcal)
1–3	1165	1230
4–6	1545	1715
7–10	1740	1970
11–14	1845	2220
15–18	2110	2755
19–49	1940	2550
50–59	1900	2550
60–64	1900	2380
65–74	1900	2330

Carbohydrates These energy-providing substances are present in varying amounts in different foods and are found in three main forms: sugars, starches and non-starch polysaccharides (NSP), usually called fibre.

There are two types of sugars: *intrinsic sugars*, which occur naturally in fruit (fructose) and sweet-tasting vegetables, and *extrinsic sugars*, which include lactose (from milk) and all the non-milk extrinsic sugars (NMEs) – sucrose (table sugar), honey, treacle, molasses and so on. The NMEs, or 'added' sugars, provide only calories, whereas foods containing intrinsic sugars also offer vitamins, minerals and fibre. Added sugars (*simple carbohydrates*) are digested and absorbed rapidly to provide energy very quickly. Starches and fibre (*complex carbohydrates*), on the other hand, break down more slowly to offer a longer-term energy source (see also Glycaemic Index). Starchy carbohydrates are found in bread, pasta, rice, wholegrain and breakfast cereals, and potatoes and other starchy vegetables such as parsnips, sweet potatoes and yams.

Healthy eating guidelines recommend that at least half of our daily energy (calories) should come from carbohydrates, and that most of this should be from complex carbohydrates. No more than 11% of our total calorie intake should come from 'added' sugars. For an average woman aged 19–49 years, this would mean a total carbohydrate intake of 259 g per day, of which 202 g should be from starch and intrinsic sugars and no more than 57 g from added sugars. For a man of the same age, total carbohydrates each day should be about 340 g (265 g from starch and intrinsic sugars and 75 g from added sugars).

See also Fibre and Glycogen.

Cholesterol There are two types of cholesterol – the soft waxy substance called blood cholesterol, which is an integral part of human cell membranes, and dietary cholesterol, which is contained in food. *Blood cholesterol* is important in the formation of some hormones and it aids digestion. High blood cholesterol levels are known to be an important risk factor for coronary heart disease, but most of the cholesterol in our blood is made by the liver – only about 25% comes from cholesterol in food. So while it would seem that the amount of cholesterol-rich foods in the diet would have a direct effect on blood cholesterol levels, in fact the best way to reduce blood cholesterol is to eat less saturated fat and to increase intake of foods containing soluble fibre.

Fat Although a small amount of fat is essential for good health, most people consume far too much. Healthy eating guidelines recommend that no more than 33% of our daily energy intake (calories) should come from fat. Each gram of fat contains 9 kcal, more than twice as many calories as carbohydrate or protein, so for a woman aged 19–49 years this means a daily maximum of 71 g fat, and for a man in the same age range 93.5 g fat.

Fats can be divided into 3 main groups: saturated, monounsaturated and polyunsaturated, depending on the chemical structure of the fatty acids they contain. *Saturated fatty acids* are found mainly in animal fats such as butter and other dairy products and in fatty meat. A high intake of saturated fat is known to be a risk factor for coronary heart disease and certain types of cancer. Current guidelines are that no more than 10% of our daily calories should come from saturated fats, which is about 21.5 g for an adult woman and 28.5 g for a man.

Where saturated fats tend to be solid at room temperature, the *unsaturated fatty acids* –

monounsaturated and polyunsaturated – tend to be liquid. *Monounsaturated fats* are found predominantly in olive oil, groundnut (peanut) oil, rapeseed oil and avocados. Foods high in *polyunsaturates* include most vegetable oils – the exceptions are palm oil and coconut oil, both of which are saturated.

Both saturated and monounsaturated fatty acids can be made by the body, but certain polyunsaturated fatty acids – known as *essential fatty acids* – must be supplied by food. There are 2 'families' of these essential fatty acids: *omega-6*, derived from linoleic acid, and *omega-3*, from linolenic acid. The main food sources of the omega-6 family are vegetable oils such as olive and sunflower; omega-3 fatty acids are provided by oily fish, nuts, and vegetable oils such as soya and rapeseed.

When vegetable oils are hydrogenated (hardened) to make margarine and reduced-fat spreads, their unsaturated fatty acids can be changed into trans fatty acids, or 'trans fats'. These artificially produced trans fats are believed to act in the same way as saturated fats within the body – with the same risks to health. Current healthy eating guidelines suggest that no more than 2% of our daily calories should come from trans fats, which is about 4.3 g for an adult woman and 5.6 g for a man. In thinking about the amount of trans fats you consume, remember that major sources are processed foods such as biscuits, pies, cakes and crisps.

Fibre Technically non-starch polysaccharides (NSP), fibre is the term commonly used to describe several different compounds, such as pectin, hemicellulose, lignin and gums, which are found in the cell walls of all plants. The body cannot digest fibre, nor does it have much nutritional value, but it plays an important role in helping us to stay healthy.

Fibre can be divided into 2 groups – soluble and insoluble. Both types are provided by most plant foods, but some foods are particularly good sources of one type or the other. *Soluble fibre* (in oats, pulses, fruit and vegetables) can help to reduce high blood cholesterol levels and to control blood sugar levels by slowing down the absorption of sugar. *Insoluble fibre* (in wholegrain cereals, pulses, fruit and vegetables) increases stool bulk and speeds the passage of waste material through the body. In this way it helps to prevent constipation, haemorrhoids and diverticular disease, and may protect against bowel cancer.

Our current intake of fibre is around 12 g a day. Healthy eating guidelines suggest that we need to increase this amount to 18 g a day.

Free radicals These highly reactive molecules can cause damage to cell walls and DNA (the genetic material found within cells). They are believed to be involved in the development of heart disease, some cancers and premature ageing. Free radicals are produced naturally by the body in the course of everyday life, but certain factors, such as cigarette smoke, pollution and over-exposure to sunlight, can accelerate their production.

Gluten A protein found in wheat and, to a lesser degree, in rye, barley and oats, but not in corn (maize) or rice. People with *coeliac disease* have a sensitivity to gluten and need to eliminate all gluten-containing foods, such as bread, pasta, cakes and biscuits, from their diet.

Glycaemic Index (GI) This is used to measure the rate at which carbohydrate foods are digested and converted into sugar (glucose) to raise blood sugar levels and provide energy. Foods with a high GI are quickly broken down and offer an immediate energy fix, while those with a lower GI are absorbed more slowly, making you feel full for longer and helping to keep blood sugar levels constant. High-GI foods include table sugar, honey, mashed potatoes and watermelon. Low-GI foods include pulses, wholewheat cereals, apples, cherries, dried apricots, pasta and oats.

Glycogen This is one of the 2 forms in which energy from carbohydrates is made available for use by the body (the other is *glucose*). Whereas glucose is converted quickly from carbohydrates and made available in the blood for a fast energy fix, glycogen is stored in the liver and muscles to fuel longer-term energy needs. When the body has used up its immediate supply of glucose, the stored glycogen is broken down into glucose to continue supplying energy.

Minerals These inorganic substances perform a wide range of vital functions in the body. The *macrominerals* – calcium, chloride, magnesium, potassium, phosphorus and sodium – are needed in relatively large quantities, whereas much smaller amounts are required of the remainder, called *microminerals*. Some microminerals (selenium, magnesium and iodine, for example) are needed in such tiny amounts that they are known as *'trace elements'*.

There are important differences in the body's ability to absorb minerals from different foods, and this can be affected by the presence of other substances. For example, oxalic acid, present in spinach, interferes with the absorption of much of the iron and calcium spinach contains.
- *Calcium* is essential for the development of strong bones and teeth. It also plays an important role in blood clotting. Good sources include dairy products, canned fish (eaten with their bones) and dark green, leafy vegetables.
- *Chloride* helps to maintain the body's fluid balance. The main source in the diet is table salt.
- *Chromium* is important in the regulation of blood sugar levels, as well as levels of fat and cholesterol in the blood. Good dietary sources include red meat, liver, eggs, seafood, cheese and wholegrain cereals.

- *Copper*, component of many enzymes, is needed for bone growth and the formation of connective tissue. It helps the body to absorb iron from food. Good sources include offal, shellfish, mushrooms, cocoa, nuts and seeds.
- *Iodine* is an important component of the thyroid hormones, which govern the rate and efficiency at which food is converted into energy. Good sources include seafood, seaweed and vegetables (depending on the iodine content of the soil in which they are grown).
- *Iron* is an essential component of haemoglobin, the pigment in red blood cells that carries oxygen around the body. Good sources are offal, red meat, dried apricots and prunes, and iron-fortified breakfast cereals.
- *Magnesium* is important for healthy bones, the release of energy from food, and nerve and muscle function. Good sources include wholegrain cereals, peas and other green vegetables, pulses, dried fruit and nuts.
- *Manganese* is a vital component of several enzymes that are involved in energy production and many other functions. Good dietary sources include nuts, cereals, brown rice, pulses and wholemeal bread.
- *Molybdenum* is an essential component of several enzymes, including those involved in the production of DNA. Good sources are offal, yeast, pulses, wholegrain cereals and green leafy vegetables.
- *Phosphorus* is important for healthy bones and teeth and for the release of energy from foods. It is found in most foods. Particularly good sources include dairy products, red meat, poultry, fish and eggs.
- *Potassium*, along with sodium, is important in maintaining fluid balance and regulating blood pressure, and is essential for the transmission of nerve impulses. Good sources include fruit, especially bananas and citrus fruits, nuts, seeds, potatoes and pulses.
- *Selenium* is a powerful antioxidant that protects cells against damage by free radicals. Good dietary sources are meat, fish, dairy foods, brazil nuts, avocados and lentils.
- *Sodium* works with potassium to regulate fluid balance, and is essential for nerve and muscle function. Only a little sodium is needed – we tend to get too much in our diet. The main source in the diet is table salt, as well as salty processed foods and ready-prepared foods.
- *Sulphur* is a component of 2 essential amino acids. Protein foods are the main source.
- *Zinc* is vital for normal growth, as well as reproduction and immunity. Good dietary sources include oysters, red meat, peanuts and sunflower seeds.

Phytochemicals These biologically active compounds, found in most plant foods, are believed to be beneficial in disease prevention. There are literally thousands of different phytochemicals, amongst which are the following:

- *Allicin*, a phytochemical found in garlic, onions, leeks, chives and shallots, is believed to help lower high blood cholesterol levels and stimulate the immune system.
- *Bioflavonoids*, of which there are at least 6000, are found mainly in fruit and sweet-tasting vegetables. Different bioflavonoids have different roles – some are antioxidants, while others act as anti-disease agents. A sub-group of these phytochemicals, called *flavonols*, includes the antioxidant *quercetin*, which is believed to reduce the risk of heart disease and help to protect against cataracts. Quercetin is found in tea, red wine, grapes and broad beans.
- *Carotenoids*, the best known of which are *beta-carotene* and *lycopene*, are powerful antioxidants thought to help protect us against certain types of cancer. Highly coloured fruits and vegetables, such as blackcurrants, mangoes, tomatoes, carrots, sweet potatoes, pumpkin and dark green, leafy vegetables, are excellent sources of carotenoids.
- *Coumarins* are believed to help protect against cancer by inhibiting the formation of tumours. Oranges are a rich source.
- *Glucosinolates*, found mainly in cruciferous vegetables, particularly broccoli, Brussels sprouts, cabbage, kale and cauliflower, are believed to have strong anti-cancer effects. *Sulphoraphane* is one of the powerful cancer-fighting substances produced by glucosinolates.
- *Phytoestrogens* have a chemical structure similar to the female hormone oestrogen, and they are believed to help protect against hormone-related cancers such as breast and prostate cancer. One of the types of these phytochemicals, called *isoflavones*, may also help to relieve symptoms associated with the menopause. Soya beans and chickpeas are a particularly rich source of isoflavones.

Protein This nutrient, necessary for growth and development, for maintenance and repair of cells, and for the production of enzymes, antibodies and hormones, is essential to keep the body working efficiently. Protein is made up of *amino acids*, which are compounds containing the 4 elements that are necessary for life: carbon, hydrogen, oxygen and nitrogen. We need all of the 20 amino acids commonly found in plant and animal proteins. The human body can make 12 of these, but the remaining 8 – called *essential amino acids* – must be obtained from the food we eat.

Protein comes in a wide variety of foods. Meat, fish, dairy products, eggs and soya beans contain all of the essential amino acids, and are therefore called first-class protein foods. Pulses, nuts, seeds and cereals are also good sources of protein, but do not contain the full range of essential amino acids. In practical terms, this really doesn't matter – as long as you include a variety of different protein foods in your diet, your body will get all the amino acids it needs. It is important, though, to eat protein foods every day because the essential amino acids cannot be stored in the body for later use.

The RNI of protein for women aged 19–49 years is 45 g per day and for men of the same age 55 g. In the UK most people eat more protein than they need, although this isn't normally a problem.

Reference Nutrient Intake (RNI)
This denotes the average daily amount of vitamins and minerals thought to be sufficient to meet the nutritional needs of almost all individuals within the population. The figures, published by the Department of Health, vary depending on age, sex and specific nutritional needs such as pregnancy. RNIs are equivalent to what used to be called Recommended Daily Amounts or Allowances (RDA).

RNIs for adults (19–49 years)

Vitamin A	600–700 mcg
Vitamin B_1	0.8 mg for women, 1 mg for men
Vitamin B_2	1.1 mg for women, 1.3 mg for men
Niacin	13 mg for women, 17 mg for men
Vitamin B_6	1.2 mg for women, 1.4 mg for men
Vitamin B_{12}	1.5 mg
Folate	200 mcg (400 mcg for first trimester of pregnancy)
Vitamin C	40 mg
Vitamin E	no recommendation in the UK; the EC RDA is 10 mg, which has been used in all recipe analyses in this book
Calcium	700 mg
Chloride	2500 mg
Copper	1.2 mg
Iodine	140 mcg
Iron	14.8 mg for women, 8.7 mg for men
Magnesium	270–300 mg
Phosphorus	550 mg
Potassium	3500 mg
Selenium	60 mcg for women, 75 mcg for men
Sodium	1600 mg
Zinc	7 mg for women, 9.5 mg for men

Vitamins These are organic compounds that are essential for good health. Although they are required in only small amounts, each one has specific vital functions to perform. Most vitamins cannot be made by the human body, and therefore must be obtained from the diet. The body is capable of storing some vitamins (A, D, E, K and B_{12}), but the rest need to be provided by the diet on a regular basis. A well-balanced diet, containing a wide variety of different foods, is the best way to ensure that you get all the vitamins you need.

Vitamins can be divided into 2 groups: *water-soluble* (B complex and C) and *fat-soluble* (A, D, E and K). Water-soluble vitamins are easily destroyed during processing, storage, and the preparation and cooking of food. The fat-soluble vitamins are less vulnerable to losses during cooking and processing.

• *Vitamin A* (retinol) is essential for healthy vision, eyes, skin and growth. Good sources include dairy products, offal (especially liver), eggs and oily fish. Vitamin A can also be obtained from *beta-carotene*, the pigment found in highly coloured fruit and vegetables. In addition to acting as a source of vitamin A, beta-carotene has an important role to play as an antioxidant in its own right.

• *The B Complex vitamins* have very similar roles to play in nutrition, and many of them occur together in the same foods.
Vitamin B_1 (thiamin) is essential in the release of energy from carbohydrates. Good sources include milk, offal, meat (especially pork), wholegrain and fortified breakfast cereals, nuts and pulses, yeast extract and wheat germ. White flour and bread are fortified with B_1 in the UK.
Vitamin B_2 (riboflavin) is vital for growth, healthy skin and eyes, and the release of energy from food. Good sources include milk, meat, offal, eggs, cheese, fortified breakfast cereals, yeast extract and green leafy vegetables.
Niacin (nicotinic acid), sometimes called vitamin B_3, plays an important role in the release of energy within the cells. Unlike the other B vitamins it can be made by the body from the essential amino acid tryptophan. Good sources include meat, offal, fish, fortified breakfast cereals and pulses. White flour and bread are fortified with niacin in the UK.
Pantothenic acid, sometimes called vitamin B_5, is involved in a number of metabolic reactions, including energy production. This vitamin is present in most foods; notable exceptions are fat, oil and sugar. Good sources include liver, kidneys, yeast, egg yolks, fish roe, wheat germ, nuts, pulses and fresh vegetables.
Vitamin B_6 (pyridoxine) helps the body to utilise protein and contributes to the formation of haemoglobin for red blood cells. B_6 is found in a wide range of foods including meat, liver, fish, eggs, wholegrain cereals, some vegetables, pulses, brown rice, nuts and yeast extract.
Vitamin B_{12} (cyanocobalamin) is vital for growth, the formation of red blood cells and maintenance of a healthy nervous system. B_{12} is unique in that it is principally found in foods of animal origin. Vegetarians who eat dairy products will get enough, but vegans need to ensure they include food fortified with B_{12} in their diet. Good sources of B_{12} include liver, kidneys, oily fish, meat, cheese, eggs and milk.
Folate (folic acid) is involved in the manufacture of amino acids and in the production of red blood cells. Recent research suggests that folate may also help to protect against heart disease. Good sources of folate are green leafy vegetables, liver, pulses, eggs, wholegrain cereal products and fortified breakfast cereals, brewers' yeast, wheatgerm, nuts and fruit, especially grapefruit and oranges.
Biotin is needed for various metabolic reactions and the release of energy from foods. Good sources include liver, oily fish, brewers' yeast, kidneys, egg yolks and brown rice.
• *Vitamin C* (ascorbic acid) is essential for growth and vital for the formation of collagen (a protein needed for healthy bones, teeth, gums, blood capillaries and all connective tissue). It plays an important role in the healing of wounds and fractures, and acts as a powerful antioxidant. Vitamin C is found mainly in fruit and vegetables.
• *Vitamin D* (cholecalciferol) is essential for growth and the absorption of calcium, and thus for the formation of healthy bones. It is also involved in maintaining a healthy nervous system. The amount of vitamin D occurring naturally in foods is small, and it is found in very few foods – good sources are oily fish (and fish liver oil supplements), eggs and liver, as well as breakfast cereals, margarine and full-fat milk that are fortified with vitamin D. Most vitamin D, however, does not come from the diet but is made by the body when the skin is exposed to sunlight.
• *Vitamin E* is not one vitamin, but a number of related compounds called tocopherols that function as antioxidants. Good sources of vitamin E are vegetable oils, polyunsaturated margarines, wheatgerm, sunflower seeds, nuts, oily fish, eggs, wholegrain cereals, avocados and spinach.
• *Vitamin K* is essential for the production of several proteins, including prothombin which is involved in the clotting of blood. It has been found to exist in 3 forms, one of which is obtained from food while the other 2 are made by the bacteria in the intestine. Vitamin K_1, which is the form found in food, is present in broccoli, cabbage, spinach, milk, margarine, vegetable oils, particularly soya oil, cereals, liver, alfalfa and kelp.

Nutritional analyses
The nutritional analysis of each recipe has been carried out using data from *The Composition of Foods* with additional data from food manufacturers where appropriate. Because the level and availability of different nutrients can vary, depending on factors like growing conditions and breed of animal, the figures are intended as an approximate guide only.

The analyses include vitamins A, B_1, B_2, B_6, B_{12}, niacin, folate, C, D and E, and the minerals calcium, copper, iron, potassium, selenium and zinc. Other vitamins and minerals are not included, as deficiencies are rare. Optional ingredients and optional serving suggestions have not been included in the calculations.

Index

index

Printing and binding: Tien Wah Press Limited, Singapore
Separations: Colour Systems Ltd, London
Paper: StoraEnso

Book code: 400-192-01
ISBN: 0 276 42801 3
Oracle Code: 250008080S.00.24